Macmillan Building and Surveying Series

Series Editor: Ivor H. Seeley
Emeritus Professor, Nottingham Trent University

BRN 35543

(continued overleaf)

D0267213

Recreation Planning and Development   Neil Ravenscroft
Resource Management for Construction   M.R. Canter
Small Building Works Management   Alan Griffith
Structural Detailing, second edition   P. Newton
Urban Land Economics and Public Policy, fourth edition
  P.N. Balchin, J.L. Kieve and G.H. Bull
Urban Renewal – Theory and Practice   Chris Couch
1980 JCT Standard Form of Building Contract, second edition
  R.F. Fellows

Series Standing Order

If you would like to receive future titles in this series as they are published, you can make use of our standing order facility. To place a standing order please contact your bookseller or, in case of difficulty, write to us at the address below with your name and address and the name of the series. Please state with which title you wish to begin your standing order. (If you live outside the United Kingdom we may not have the rights for your area, in which case we will forward your order to the publisher concerned.)

Customer Services Department, Macmillan Distribution Ltd
Houndmills, Basingstoke, Hampshire, RG21 2XS, England.

Resource Management
for Construction
An integrated approach

M.R. Canter

M. Phil., M.C.I.O.B.
Principal Lecturer
Head of Building Technology & Management
Division – B.E.S.T. Faculty
Anglia Polytechnic University

MACMILLAN

First published 1993 by
THE MACMILLAN PRESS LTD
Houndmills, Basingstoke, Hampshire RG21 2XS
and London
Companies and representatives
throughout the world

ISBN 0–333–55254–7

690·068

044466

£15·39 iR

A catalogue record for this book is available
from the British Library

Contents

Preface

This book has been produced as a result of my particular interest in small building companies and their management problems. Many of the ideas presented were developed when I was carrying out research into cashflow management and how this might be achieved by the smaller company.

Cashflow should be seen as the culmination of the acquisition and usage of resources, on the one hand, and the payment by a client/customer for a service or product resulting from value added to the resources employed, on the other.

If managers organise and use the resources at their disposal effectively, then it is reasonable to argue that the eventual cashflows on projects become more balanced, and therefore better planned for and managed.

Small construction companies make up by far the largest sector of the construction industry, and it is the survival and growth of such companies that should be seen as vitally important from an economic standpoint.

In chapter 1 the nature and structure of the case study company are presented, so that the problems of resource management faced by the industry can be examined. This company was one of the many studied by the author and typifies the type of small general construction organisation operating in the industry today.

The description of how this company operates and the problems it faces has been used as a vehicle for the application of general management theory and practice to situations derived from the internal and external operational environments which have a direct affect on resource management, and from this cost control and eventual cashflow.

As stated in the introduction to chapter 1, this book has two main aims. The first is to provide a clear text dealing with the relationship between resource management and cost management for students on construction courses. Underlying this first aim is the provision of a theme to their studies, so that relationships are better understood.

The second aim is the provision of an easy-to-use reference book for busy managers seeking to improve their resource organisation and management.

Each chapter commences with a statement of chapter aims and finishes with a summary of the ideas presented.

The early chapters examine the problems of resource control, highlighting the economic, financial, social and legal pressures under which management decisions are taken. From the examination of how the individual resources might be organised and managed, the later chapters seek to demonstrate how resource costs can be classified in a structured fashion and monitored regularly so that control is exercised.

The final chapter describes how an integrated system of cost and cashflow management can be operated.

Although this book describes what might be called administrative procedures, it should not be forgotten that people are the most important resource in any organisation, and that any management procedures adopted by companies should be seen to improve the decision-making capabilities of managers and to make their lives and the lives of the people they employ more satisfying.

Witham, Essex   M.R. Canter
1993

Acknowledgements

Firstly, I must thank my wife and children for putting up with me while this book was being produced. I must also acknowledge the help and suggestions received from colleagues and students of Anglia Polytechnic University.

I am indebted to the many small companies who have allowed me access to study their procedures and to test my ideas in their organisations.

Special thanks must go to Professor Ivor Seeley for his encouragement and advice during the preparation of the book.

The author and publishers wish to thank the following for permission to use copyright material: Butterworth–Heinemann Ltd for Fig. 4.3 from *Introduction to Building Management*, 3rd ed., by R. E. Calvert, 1977; The Chartered Institute of Management Accountants for Fig. 10.3 from *Accounting in the Construction Industry* by P. Padget, 1991.

Every effort has been made to trace all the copyright holders, but if any have been inadvertently overlooked the publishers will be pleased to make the necessary arrangement at the first opportunity.

1 Introduction

This book has two principal aims. The first is to provide a clear text dealing with the relationship between resource management and cost control for students on construction courses. The second is to provide an easy-to-use reference book for managers seeking to improve their administration systems via an integrated approach to cost and resource control. If the relationships which exist between information employed in each of a company's information systems are clearly identified and understood, a manager is armed with a potentially more powerful decision-making tool than if each of the systems is considered to be a separate entity.

The following example illustrates this point. The cost of building a half-brick wall in facing bricks is found to be outside an established budget. This situation is typical of many jobs, and a manager is faced with the task of identifying the reasons for such an overspend. Of course there can be a multitude of reasons in reality; however, let us look at some of the possibilities:

- The labour output used by the estimator is unrealistic, given the nature of the work on site.
- The cost of the bricks is higher than allowed for in the estimate.
- There has been a variation to the work which has not been covered by a written instruction.

The output problem will come to light if information extracted from an on-site monitoring system is related to data presented in an estimate. The purchasing problem will be identified if a good communication channel exists between the buying, estimating and management functions. The variation issue requires the comparison of the work actually carried out with that originally proposed. Each or all of the above could have a bearing upon the cost variance, and it is up to the manager to judge the level of importance which each factor may have had and from this to take a decision to suit a given situation. If the above factors can be drawn together and examined within a cost/value reconciliation system (see chapter 11), then it should be possible to assess the relative effect that an individual factor might have, or in fact the effect that a group of factors might be having, and this should enable the manager to make more informed judgements.

It is very important that the benefits gained from operating such an integrated approach should outweigh the cost of operation, and it will be an aim to demonstrate this wherever possible.

Each chapter examines a systematic approach to the management and control of the key resources employed in a building organisation. A case study approach has been adopted as a means of examining the problems faced by an average building company. The case study company will be used as a vehicle for the application of general management theory and practice to situations derived from the internal and external operating environments which have a direct effect upon resource management and hence cost control.

It is probably true that the 'average' building company does not exist; however, many companies face similar problems and have similar levels of expertise with which to manage situations that they encounter. The basis for the description of the case study company and the way in which it operates comes from a research project carried out by the author in 1988.

Case study company

Company age

The company is comparatively young in that it was formed within the past ten years. Research has shown that building companies generally tend to be 'young' for many reasons, but some basic causes will now be identified:

- The ease with which companies can be formed and dispanded in the construction industry.
- The need to sustain and manage diversified workload together with the varying degrees of risk attached to funding and subsequently waiting for clients to pay for the work done.
- Many companies grow and in so doing change the nature of their business via diversification.

Classification and employment

The company is a general building company with a variety of work being carried out and managed. The company has four working directors together with supervisory and administrative staff employed on a full- and part-time basis. Coupled with in-house staff, use is made of consultancy services for accounting, surveying and estimating functions.

From the above, three points can be highlighted with reference to resource and cost control. Firstly, the background and training of the working directors are important. If they are involved with resource and cost management, they must have the training and aptitude to perform these functions efficiently. Secondly, in any administrative situation continuity is very important. Paperwork which is the responsibility of only one individual and which is continually moving within a system gives rise to the danger of orders/invoices etc. awaiting attention being overlooked. This is a particular problem where part-time staff or consultants are employed. Finally, people need to become involved in the work and produce information in a consistent form, in line with company requirements. Clearly these are three difficult areas, however the need to bear these important points in mind when considering the efficiency of a control system must be stressed.

The company employs fewer than 25 full-time employees and uses labour-only and labour-and-materials sub-contractors to make up the rest of its labour resource needs. This reflects market conditions, where highly variable turnover levels necessitate regular employment adjustments. From the above, two areas of financial administration will be of concern. Firstly the payroll system operated and how information from this can be related to contract costs, and secondly the administration of sub-contractors' accounts and how these relate to final accounts on contracts.

The managing director is the direction-giving force and is, together with the board of directors, responsible to the shareholders for all the company's operations. The company secretary is responsible for reporting the financial affairs of the company. He decides, in conjunction with the managing director, how the accounting systems will operate. As the board takes decisions and while work is being carried out, an internal financial monitoring system is a vital tool for measuring company performance. The board, and in particular the managing director, need to be made aware of the financial consequences of the decisions they have taken.

Operational management

There are numerous areas of the company's activities that will have an effect upon its success. However few managers would disagree with the following key operational factors, listed in order of importance:

- Maintaining the quality of the work.
- Controlling the costs of contracts.
- Ensuring that payments are received on time.

The links between these priorities and possible cashflow considerations are now pursued along with the identification of perceived operational problems.

There are two persistent problem areas for this company: obtaining payments from clients and labour acquisition, that is obtaining labour of suitable quality.

Two other areas are singled out as associated problems: the acquisition of suitable work and administration generally, and in respect of legislation in particular.

There is a clear link between the standard of labour employed and the quality of delivered contracts. The cost effects of employing inadequately trained operatives are twofold. Firstly, supervision might well need to increase as labour quality decreases. Secondly, a 'quality control' cost is likely to be encountered whereby either the cost of carrying out the work increases or there is a 'corrective element' cost where work below an acceptable standard is rejected.

Given the difficulties mentioned above, the identification of costs which are non-recoverable (such as those arising from defective work) as opposed to those which are recoverable (such as those arising from client variations) requires careful monitoring.

Clients will be reluctant to pay for work until it is shown to be of acceptable quality, and might well query payments for extra work unless it is clearly justified, identified and the extra cost set out in detail.

Three key elements should be considered in connection with overdue payments. The first is the identification of the point at which a payment became overdue. Next, possible reasons why payment is late, for example it could be a component of a bulk payment which is not yet due. Finally, the point at which payments become unacceptably late should be established. How this company approaches debt control and the attitude to 'bad debts' will have a bearing not only on contract cashflow but also on overall company cashflow levels.

The acquisition of suitable work can also be linked to the above discussion. Reputation and price are important selection criteria for clients selecting builders to carry out work. Reputation is normally built up via a network of clients who have been satisfied with the quality and price paid for work in the past. The builder's costs in achieving this quality/price mix may well affect the competitiveness of some companies. Companies operating in highly competitive markets where margins are slim may face financial administration problems. The smaller the margin between 'cost' and 'value' the more critical a company's management accounting system becomes.

The work and its problems

As stated earlier, the company is a general building company and carries out the following types of work:

- Extensions and alterations.
- Repairs and maintenance.
- Refurbishment.
- New contracts other than housing.
- New housing work (i.e. other than company-initiated speculative housing).
- New speculative (own)-housing, e.g. developments designed, constructed and financed by the company.
- New speculative (own)-shops/offices, etc.

It seems reasonable to suggest that companies who have gained considerable experience of a particular type of work should also have gained an awareness of the nature of the problems associated with that work, and also how these might be overcome. It is from new or intermittently carried out work that unusual problems might arise, and this can cause pressure to be exerted on a company's finances. Particular problem areas for the case study company with respect to resources are:

- Refurbishment.
- New non-housing contracts.
- Repair and maintenance.

Two common factors apply to the above types of work which can cause administrative problems for a builder. Firstly to appreciate the scope of the work at the tender stage and how this is defined and set out on drawings and in specifications, and secondly how to control the amount of work and its quality while a job is running.

With some types of work the total extent of the operations may not be clearly known at the outset. Also, it is common practice for clients or their representatives to change the nature of the work as it proceeds. All standard forms of contract seek to identify these risks and apportion responsibility for them. If a non-standard form of contract is used then it would be prudent to set out a method for categorising variations, into those impossible to assess at the tender stage and those occasioned by change of client's requirements.

In order that the cost of extra work, which might be recoverable or non-recoverable, is identified at an early stage, an efficient set of monitoring and measurement procedures is vital. If a client is required to pay for extra work it is important to gain agreement, preferably before the work is carried out. If the cost is non-recoverable, then its effect upon contract profit levels should be established as soon as possible.

The company carries out up to ten large contracts (values in excess of £1 000 000) in any trading period, with the rest of its turnover being made up of small works and jobbing work with values up to £50 000. The majority of the company's workload is accounted for by a large number of different customers, thus making it difficult to get to know clients and their peculiarities over short periods of time. However it is worth pointing out here the dangers of getting to know clients too well. The first danger may well be complacency, whereby clients are allowed to get away with 'paying late'. There may also be a psychological contract built up. The client, with the hint of more work in the offing, is able to take advantage of a builder in both the negotiating and payment spheres. Another danger could occur for a company carrying out fewer than ten contracts, a high proportion of which is for one client, and this client becomes a slow payer. This situation is likely to cause a knock-on effect on all the other contracts, and could be the start of serious financial difficulties if not managed effectively.

Competition and the acquisition of work

There are three very important criteria for the acquisition of work:

* Recommendations from past customers.
* Inclusion on tender lists.
* Personal contacts.

Research has shown that these three factors are seen as the most important by companies [1]. Clearly these three criteria are linked and are associated with a company's perceived track record and financial status.

The company faces competition from companies of a similar nature to itself and from larger, more sophisticated organisations when tendering for larger contracts. It is difficult to assess the level of competition in any of the construction markets within which the company operates because of the commercial nature of the information required to be collected and analysed. However where the company is in competition for work (either 'open' or 'selective' tendering situations) then its success rate ranges from winning 1 in 6 to 1 in 10 contracts.

The company also tries to be selective in the work that it prices, either trying to negotiate as 'sole tenderers' where possible or attempting to get involved with as much 'term contracting' as possible, and thus in both cases minimising competition and increasing potential workloads. There are also situations where the company faces what might be termed unfair competition in that 'winning tenders' were far too low to be realistic. This implies that at-cost or below-cost pricing might be occurring, with competing companies attempting to 'buy work'. Faced with a high level of competition and the possibility that some unfair competition might exist, what alternatives are open to the company?

If possible the company should become more selective in the work it prices, moving into markets where the potential for higher profit margins exist. This is clearly dependent upon the availability of work in the various markets and the ability of the company to secure a position within a market. It could attempt to increase the number of tenders priced, thereby trying to improve its success rates. This would have an affect upon the estimating overhead and in the long term might not prove productive.

In order to maintain or increase turnover the company can either reduce its costs and thereby prices offered to clients, or if it wishes to maintain employment and administrative levels, make offers which may not be achievable in terms of 'cost' and therefore 'value' in the short term.

In each of these situations, the company will need to be able initially to measure the level of competition and from this the potential returns from the work it carries out. It should be in a position to assess its ability to adjust workloads and the consequences of such adjustments to suit market conditions. At the very least, the company should make an assessment of the 'cost' of 'buying' work and its effect upon company finances as a whole.

Cooke [2] discusses a company's ability to monitor its tendering performance and from this its position in a market place under a concept called *bidding theory*. This approach, together with the concept of tender/estimate analysis, is pursued further in chapter 9 where the integration of estimating information with that of cost control data is discussed.

As the margin between 'cost' and 'value' on contracts gets smaller, financial control becomes critical. An important fact that appears not to be understood by all companies is that their offer when accepted by a customer becomes the cost/value measurement focus.

Financial management

The company attempts to forecast its workload on a yearly basis. A turnover forecast is also applied to this workload estimate. Clearly this does not constitute what might be termed corporate planning, however it does mean that there is a starting point from which the company can set its trading objectives and against which achievement measurements can be made.

Estimating can be seen as the starting point for the company's financial control procedures. The estimator produces a forecast of cost which when incorporated as part of a tender becomes an offer to a client to carry out work. The company's ability to recover money in excess of the offer made will be limited to the agreement made at the contract stage and will normally be controlled by contractual conditions. The actual costs on contracts must therefore be compared with estimated costs, and this provides a measurement medium which will be central to any cost control system. A clear link can be seen between an estimate and cashflow on contracts. Figure 9.1 in chapter 9 illustrates the link between estimating, cost control and cashflow.

A company's approach to the way it produces an estimate will have a great deal to do with the information upon which the estimate is to be based and the data used to produce a cost forecast. Where the information supplied (by architect or others) is sufficient (drawings, specification and/or a bill of quantities) then an analytical approach is adopted by the estimator. Where less information is provided by the client or his representatives, estimates are produced on either an operational or on a time and materials basis.

There is also a need to employ performance data to produce an estimate. The main sources of such information are:

- Experience of past contracts.
- Analysis of costs on past contracts and projecting these into the future (both of these require a reasonable level of administration and feedback from jobs).
- Price books/published sources (great care should be exercised when using these sources and a good feedback mechanism is essential for the successful use of such aids).

Whatever approach is used, two factors should be borne in mind. Firstly consideration must be given to the 'accuracy' of the data used, and if adjustments are made at tender stage, the possible consequences; and secondly, to how the data are stored, updated and retrieved in time for efficient use.

The estimate can be seen as the starting point for the company's cashflow considerations, initially for a contract and then through a series of contracts to company cashflow as a whole. The appropriateness of the data used is significant not just for winning work, but must also be seen as important for controlling cost, the flow of money and resources in general.

The company does attempt to apply a check upon the accuracy of its estimates on each of its contracts. In order for cost control to be meaningfully carried out such a check is essential. The design and use of a simple system which allows the accuracy of estimates to be assessed is seen as desirable by the company and forms part of its 'cost/value' comparison system.

If the company is to monitor profit or loss on a regular basis, 'cost/value' comparisons are very important and should be carried out regularly. The company approaches comparisons in two ways: it produces monthly reports and also operates on a management by exception basis in that it carries out comparisons when it is felt that there is a problem requiring investigation.

Finally, the company attempts to produce regular cashflow forecasts against its expected workload. The company recognises the main reasons for producing such forecasts. The most important is as a medium for monitoring present and future finance needs. Cashflow forecasts are also used as part of the company's case when seeking to obtain finance.

In the previous trading period the company has had serious pressure placed upon its cash reserves. The reasons identified for such pressure were:

- Clients delaying payments.
- Suppliers requiring prompt payment.
- Retention monies being held for long periods.
- Excessively fluctuating workloads.
- Inaccuracy of estimates.

The important factors to bear in mind are how quickly the company realises that pressure exists and what the possible consequences are.

The factors associated with cash pressure in the present case can be divided into problems with receipt of money or outflow of money to creditors and those resulting from sudden fluctuations in workload.

Refurbishment was identified as a particular problem area for the company. New contracts other than housing were singled out as also giving rise to cashflow problems, together with repairs and maintenance. The major problem with each of these types of work is that of measuring the extent of the final product. As each contract proceeds, either the work is expanded owing to unforeseen circumstances or variations are required by the client or his representatives.

In order to alleviate such situations where cashflow is a potential problem, the company adopts the following remedies in the short term:

- Using overdraft facilities to fund short-term needs and to plug gaps in inflow.
- Delaying payments to creditors.

Where either approach is used, the importance of planning repayments and identifying when creditors *must* be paid cannot be over-stressed.

Individual contracts and their administration

The company makes an attempt to calculate the financial requirements of each of its projects separately, on a regular basis. It also makes regular forecasts of the resources (labour, materials and plant) required. It is important to apply a cost forecast to the resource estimates and then attempt systematically to compare the forecasted cost with actual cost for each resource component.

If the company is to produce and monitor cashflow in a meaningful way, then the above assessments and comparisons are prerequisites.

Summary

It is intended to use the case study company as the model for the development of the management practices discussed in each of the following chapters. However it is useful also to identify some of the traits that exist in the industry in general and which might have an effect upon companies in particular.

The ease with which companies can be formed, grow and disband is an inherent aspect of the construction industry. The work carried out by the general contractor is highly varied and it is reasonable to assume that the longer a company has been trading, the better the working knowledge of markets operating within the industry, and of the administrative problems associated with different types of work.

Companies operating in multi-product/service markets may well have to adopt a variety of approaches in managing their diversified workloads. Problems may well exist for company managements with minimal expertise, and this could well be the case for a high proportion of small companies who are controlled by a small number of working directors with minimal in-house or external assistance.

There are clear links between the maintenance of quality on contracts, controlling costs and the receipt of payments. It may cost companies much more than was anticipated at the tender stage to achieve client satisfaction, and slow payment may well result if this outcome is not achieved. The acquisition of work is also associated with this requirement. Reputation and price are important selection criteria for clients. Reputation will normally be built up via a network of clients who have been satisfied with the quality and price paid for work. A builder's costs in achieving a quality/price mix may affect the competitiveness of the company. Companies operating in highly competitive markets where margins are slim may face financial administration problems.

The following chapters seek to examine the management systems necessary to manage the resources employed by the case study company efficiently.

2   Resources and Control

Introduction

The aim of this chapter is to examine the external environment within which the case study company operates, highlighting the economic, financial, social and legal pressures under which management decisions are taken. From this examination the company's existing internal management environment is reviewed in the light of the need to react to external and internal pressures.

The need to plan, coordinate, monitor, control and review activities on a regular basis, as well as for a contingency approach to the management of resources and cost, is examined using appropriate practical examples.

Management control in reality

There are many factors which are outside a manager's control, such as government policies, weather conditions, strikes in other industries, etc. It must therefore be understood that an industrial manager will never have absolute 'foot on the accelerator' control. Management control is progressive and involves continually making adjustments to the perceived possibilities of the situation as a whole, after making comparisons between planned and actual results.

Managers are therefore required to create an internal company environment which enables decisions to be made and jobs to be performed in the light of the need for the company to survive and grow.

All companies operate in an uncertain world. It is therefore essential to identify the uncertainties in any given operational situation and from this make an assessment of the level of risk involved.

The following list identifies some of the uncertainties which can arise in a typical development project:

- Scope of the work – known/unknown at tender stage.
- Site difficulties – site obstructions/roadworks/drainage/limited space.
- Availability of resources – named/unnamed goods/services – local/national position.
- Inflation – national problem.
- Productivity (efficiency) – management/operatives/methods of operation.
- Labour relations – national situation/company relations.
- Liquidity – client/contractor.
- Extent/nature of likely variations – changes in the scope of the work and possible time scales.
- Weather conditions – contract duration/time of year/position of project/site.
- Fire/damage – an insured uncertainty/risk.
- Competence of design team – supply of information.

This list is clearly not exhaustive but is indicative of the criteria that management must attempt to measure or consider when tendering for work.

There are two distinct project variants, each carrying differing uncertainty/risk problems:

(1) Speculative projects – where a builder acquires some land and builds with a view to selling the development for a estimated return.
(2) Contracting – where a builder tenders for work and either does the building himself or manages the building process for a client/employer.

There are variations on the above, but the important thing is the level of control a manager is able to exert over the internal and external uncertainties of the development system.

With (1) a building company makes a decision to develop in line with market potential. For example, in an expanding market for a particular product or service (cars, electrical goods, financial services, etc.) there will clearly be a measurable demand for the facilities to produce such products or to carry out a service. The management of the building company will make a decision based upon its measurement of potential demand for such facilities. It can therefore be said that managers in this situation will be in control of the intelligence-gathering exercise and thus should have more ability to control events (uncertainties/risks) than the managers in (2). For example, in (2) an investor (client/employer) must first make the decision to invest. From this will come the need for facilities, which will then normally be conceived and designed by a team employed by the client. Managers of building companies in this case will not be centrally involved in the intelligence-gathering process and therefore their ability to control events is diminished. Ability to control events is in line with the level of involvement with the intelligence-gathering functions.

Generally speaking, building companies are normally one or two steps away from the original investment decision. This also means that they are generally removed from:

- The original choice of basic resources and how they might be best employed.
- The decision to produce or supply the basic resources required for the development process.

As can be seen from the discussion above, management decision-making will of necessity need to take cognisance of factors either within a development scenario, company system or in fact an economic environment.

The market mechanism

Building companies not only operate within an economic environment, but they also provide the facilities and services upon which economic activity is sustained. It is therefore important that building managers appreciate how investment decisions are taken within a particular economic system at any given time. The time aspect is very important, as can be clearly seen from a study of economic activity in Britain over a period which covers two governments of different political outlooks. Economists identify three basic types of economy, namely:

- The command economy where central government attempts to plan economic activity allowing little or no free enterprise and with industry under government control. Governments in this situation are in a position to direct what is to be produced and also how it is produced. This type of economic system prevailed in Eastern Europe for approximately 70 years, until the late 1980s when dramatic political change influenced the introduction of a more market-orientated approach to economic decision-making.
- The free economy where central government does not interfere with business activity and allows a free enterprise system to operate unfettered. This type of economic system is also called a market

economy and within such a system some economists argue that the 'price' of goods (in our case resources) brings about a balance between the demand for such goods and the supply of these by business. In such a *laissez-faire* system it becomes very difficult for managers to plan the acquisition and use of resources on a long-term basis.

- The mixed economy which bridges the gap between the above two extremes and predominates in Britain and the majority of countries in the world in the 1990s. In such an economy one can clearly see government intervention in the form of:

    Taxation

    Control of interest rates

    Issuing of grants and subsidies

    each of which either encourages or discourages investment. It is investment that ultimately has a bearing upon the nature of the resources employed in any industry. There is clearly more scope to plan the deployment and use of resources over longer periods in mixed economies which exhibit growth trends.

The nature of resources

In order to evaluate the type and quantity of any resource required to be used it will be necessary to examine the type and level of demand within a particular market. As demand changes then clearly resource needs change. A major problem in the resource-planning exercise is that there are varying degrees of flexibility attached to resources. The following examples illustrate this idea:

- Land cannot be moved, and in order to change the nature of land or building usage a great deal of effort and time might be required. Aspects such as demolition, design/planning approvals and building control sanctions all have to be considered before change in use can be achieved. Land is also a finite resource and cannot be increased; only when planning authorities change the designation of land usage is there an opportunity to increase the capacity of land for building purposes.
- Labour (operational/managerial) – varying degrees of flexibility exist here. Clearly people can move physically to different areas where they may be needed to work. However there are a number of obstacles which may hinder the smooth movement of personnel, and management must understand and take account of such factors when considering manpower planning. Some of the factors are identified here to illustrate the management problems:

(1) Individuals may not wish to move to a new area because of family ties or commitments. Managers responsible for and to individuals must also understand that even if people do move to new areas there may still be psychological/sociological problems associated with such moves, and that such factors must be taken into account within the planning equation.

(2) The cost of moving for the individual or the company may well be prohibitive and clearly there is a need to analyse the cost consequences from both standpoints realistically.

(3) Skill is an important determinant in the manpower equation. New demands (technological/managerial) mean that the skills possessed by a workforce may become obsolete. Management can either decide to buy such new skills/expertise into the organisation or plan to train people to meet new demands dictated by market forces. Both options will require the time and cost implications to be carefully considered.

- Materials/plant are considered together here because they both have similar control problems for management. Materials or machines can generally be produced or manufactured anywhere if a convenient production unit can be sited. However, some materials, such as aggregates, have to be refined or manufactured close to the place where they are naturally extracted. The main areas where control problems arise for both resource groups are:

    (1) Transportation
    (2) Quality and quality management
    (3) Quantity and stock control
    (4) Wastage and productivity
    (5) Reconciliation of intentions with actual performance.

- Capital (long term/working capital) in its various forms really enables a company to carry out its objectives. It is constantly changing in nature, for example cash enables resources to be acquired which in turn become work-in-progress, which eventually is valued as finished stock and the income received from valuations provides cash to start the cycle again. The major problem for a company is what is sometimes termed *capital lock-up*. This will be examined in detail in chapter 11, but briefly capital deployed in a particular way, within say a contractual arrangement, becomes locked into that arrangement and cannot be readily used for other purposes.

Having examined the nature and constraints upon resources within a market system, it is appropriate to examine the problems encountered by the case study company in the markets in which it operates.

Market structure

It is well known that the construction industry is made up of a large number of diverse organisations [3]. They can either be classified as general (the case study company) or specialist under a description of their trade, such as plumbers, painters, etc. In contrast to many other industries which exhibit long-term trends towards higher levels of concentration and domination by large multi-divisional organisations [4], the influence of small firms in the construction industry has increased both in terms of numbers and share of output over the years [5, 6]. The largest and most fragmented grouping is the specialist trades, with civil engineering companies being the smallest, and general builders falling between these two groups.

The fragmented structure of the construction industry is not unique to Britain [3]. The basic nature of construction reflects the economics of production, which tend to favour small companies organised by specialisms. The two most important features of production which set construction apart from most manufacturing industries are:

(1) The immobility of production. The company has to find the customer, who will require the work to be carried out at his convenience. Each site will be a temporary place of work requiring a temporary organisation to be set up every time.
(2) Virtually every job is specific and individual, requiring a diversity of skills, often provided by specialists on a sub-contract basis.

These factors tend to reduce the scope for economies of scale which large-scale centralised production units might achieve. Having said this, there have been many instances of industrialisation of production in the construction industry [7]. An example of this is the use of timber frame components produced under factory conditions and then delivered to site for assembly. This assembly exercise has diminished the requirements for the traditionally skilled craft operative and as such has placed more emphasis on the management of a relatively simplified erection process. This being the case, and bearing in mind the limited scope for the introduction of industrialisation across the industry as a whole, generally the smaller company (case study company) is not at a competitive disadvantage when pricing against the larger company in terms of the basic operations on site. The areas where a larger company is likely to have a competitive edge over its smaller counterpart are those of resources available and management expertise.

Regardless of whether a house, office, factory or shop is being built, many individual functions are required to be carried out. This has led over the centuries to specialisation of functions which are classified by trade rather than by building attribute. This has reinforced the tendency to organise site operations around small-scale trade-based activities involving specialists for relatively small parts of any contract. These aspects of specialisation and small work packages have been instrumental in the development and growth of sub-contracting within the industry.

There are a number of contributory factors why general contractors will sub-let varying degrees of their contract work. Specialisation by type of construction work makes companies more vulnerable to fluctuations in demand. Generally the demand for particular types of work is less stable than for construction work as a whole. Specialisation by sub-contractors enables them to build up expertise and experience, bringing with both the possibilities of enhanced productivity. A sub-contractor generally has the advantage of being able to maintain a labour force intact by moving from one project to another, as opposed to the main contractor who may have to reduce his labour force in line with company workload. This of course would depend upon the main contractor's area of operations and his ability to acquire work, in line with employment levels. There is also a possible benefit to the sub-contractor of easier management control, which should be simplified by the concentration on a particular specialism. The above considerations will apply to large and small general contractors alike.

The large number of small companies, together with the absence of entry or exit barriers and limited scope for collusion, tends to make construction a very competitive industry. Low barriers to entry are a consequence of the industry's limited capital requirements. Given the mobility of the company's organisation rather than the product, building companies do not require large premises – the need is for a head office to provide essential administrative services to site organisations which move from site to site. Much of the capital equipment needed on sites is available from an extensive plant hire sector [8]. Because of the nature of many building processes, being craft based and labour intensive, the scope for large-scale plant usage on contracts is constrained. However plant hire has increased the ability of the small builder to compete with the large company. Working capital requirements are also low, generally because stage payments through the life of a contract are the norm, with further aid to short-term financing being provided via trade credit facilities.

Finally, it is difficult for individual contractors to exert any significant control over the markets in which they operate because of a number of economic and contractual factors. The first is the high level of competitive tendering necessary for most companies to win a share of contracts, the volume and size of which are difficult to predict. Secondly, even when a company carries out its own speculative work, the price which it is able to sell a building for will be influenced to a large extent by the price of similar properties in the vicinity [8]. Building companies, whether large or small, generally have to react to the demands of the market, and the company which makes an effort to monitor the requirements of its particular market sectors may be able to be more competitive than companies which do not.

Response to potential demand

A number of factors will combine to influence the way in which the construction industry responds to demands for its products or services. Such factors can be summarised as follows:

(1) Construction output takes place on a fixed site and such sites, although widely spread throughout the country, are likely to be clustered in regions where potential demand for construction services emerge.
(2) The materials and components used in construction are normally heavy, thus making transport costs prohibitive if distances required to be travelled are great. The problem of transporting labour large distances to sites is also not cost effective, making the employment of local labour and local sub-contractors more desirable. For similar reasons it is desirable to use local materials suppliers where possible.
(3) The labour content of most building work is high. The difficulties in supervising labour from a distance are well documented [3, 8, 9], again making the employment of supervisors and managers who are familiar with localities and are based locally advantageous.
(4) Investment in and consumption of construction services are based upon industrial and commercial trends which are affected by governmental (central and local) influences, and both have a bearing on households. In Britain there has been a tendency for investment and consumption to be concentrated in the south and south-east regions [5], thus emphasising the regional nature of demand and supply. In the early 1990s there was a marginal shift in this trend.

As a consequence of the above factors the industry is structured such that, except for large contracts, work tends to be carried out within a radius of no more than 50 miles (80 km) from a builder's office, with the small company operating within a 10 to 20 mile (15 to 30 km) radius of the office.

In summary, the size and geographical spread of demand for building work calls for a special type of relationship between a builder and a client. With small repair and maintenance work, the most important considerations are likely to be speed and reliability. A client, whether industrial or domestic, will attempt to choose a company that can provide a quick reliable service. The small local company is an obvious choice. They are easily contacted, readily available and usually carry out the work relatively quickly. A continuing relationship is likely to develop between both parties if, firstly, the work is carried out satisfactorily and, secondly, the client honours the commitment to pay for the work. For new construction work the client in the private sector is usually in the market for work to be carried out only once, and then for a very expensive item. As a consequence the emphasis might be placed more on price than reputation, although reputation will still be an important consideration. The client is trying to select a builder with a good reputation and who is not too expensive. Here again, a local builder who operates within a limited radius of the home base will win a large proportion of his work by personal recommendation. Irrespective of how much or of what type of work a company undertakes, a builder needs to establish a good knowledge of the markets it operates in plus a reputation for carrying out specific types of work efficiently.

The problem for any building company is that not only is the industry a diverse one but it is also subject to dynamic changes in type and level of demand brought about by investment and consumption preferences. There is therefore a need for companies to be flexible in their approach to markets. Allied to this the general builder may well be able to establish a good reputation for carrying out varied types of work, thus not only becoming well known in a local market, but also gaining considerable knowledge of diversified markets.

Summary

In conclusion, it is relatively easy to enter the general building market. New housing work and repair and maintenance both require little advanced technical skills [8, 10], thus enabling companies to be set up by those with very little specialist training or indeed with no building industry experience [1, 10]. The capital required to start up a company in the building industry is quite low. Small new projects and maintenance work do not require extensive use of plant. Materials are usually provided by suppliers on credit. Labour requires payment each week, and finance is required up to the point of payment receipt. The same is true of sub-contractors. On small contracts this will be no more than, say, two to four weeks. In the case of larger contracts, payment by the client is normally via a stage payment system where the work is valued at the end of a month and payment should be forthcoming before the end of the next month. It is only on the larger contracts where finance becomes more of a problem. Where companies are operating at a relatively consistent turnover level, payments from previous contracts can be utilised to finance current operations. The major problems occur when a company attempts to expand at a faster rate than can be resourced or when credit facilities are withdrawn creating financial difficulties. Not only is it easy to enter the industry but it is also very easy to leave, either by enforced or voluntary liquidation caused by financial pressure.

Thus the factors which give rise to the prominence of small general building companies (the case study company in particular) are:

(1) Their ability to be flexible and take on a diversified workload to suit demand potential in a locality.
(2) A general rather than a specialised knowledge of building operations is a help in the provision of a varied service or product to different types of client.
(3) There is no requirement to finance the provision of capital-intensive resources. Credit provisions and the work itself provide the necessary working capital for operations. This last point applies to the majority of small building companies.

The most important determinant factor in what happens to the small company sector of the industry is what happens to the demand for work in general and in particular markets.

The attributes of the small general building company appear to make this type of organisation well suited to respond to changing demand. A major factor when considering a small company's ability to maintain or increase its share in a highly dynamic changing industry is how it approaches the administration and management of its workload, and the resources that go to make up the service provided to clients. A particular problem that companies need to get to grips with is the financial administration and management of diversified order books.

3 Manpower Management

Introduction

There is clearly a need to identify activities to be carried out and methods to be employed, and then to fit the 'right' type of management and labour to an operation. That will be the theme of this chapter.

There are two aspects of manpower deployment to consider:

- Operational.
- Managerial.

It must not be forgotten that there is a quality aspect associated with manpower, which is very difficult to measure. However, skills and expertise can be identified within individuals. Such factors are continually changing to suit the needs of industry. Companies are faced with a compelling need to employ manpower that is not only suitably qualified but also flexible enough to add to or change their experience base to meet the demands of a rapidly changing economic environment. Apart from being required to assess a company's current manpower needs, managers will also need to produce and update a manpower plan. Companies face a choice. They can train their existing personnel in line with a set of objectives within their manpower plan – this clearly has time and cost consequences associated with it. Alternatively, personnel can be 'bought-in', an approach that has not only cost implications, but also organisational and motivational consequences.

The aim of this chapter is to examine how both managerial and operational personnel are employed and then deployed in line with a set of objectives detailed in a manpower plan.

Activity analysis

There are two aspects of activity analysis:

Objectives
Activity evaluation

These two aspects are central to any manpower planning exercise.
When activity objectives are examined it should be possible to identify the following:

- Is the activity really necessary?
- Why does the activity need to be carried out?
- When does it need to be carried out?
- What relationships exist between this activity and other activities?

These may well seem very basic and obvious questions. However it is interesting to note how many activities in a small building company were traditionally carried out by a particular individual in a particular way [10]. Companies rarely review how they operate until something goes wrong, and quite often this is too late.

Before changing the way things are done it is important to understand the existing situation and to make improvements with a clear knowledge of constraints and relationships. It does not really matter who carries out an activity so long as the capacity exists to perform it adequately – it is the achieving of a business objective that is the key issue. For example, a site manager may wish to know how much it is costing to place concrete in beams. It is of no concern who produces the information so long as the data is reliable, relevant and produced in time to be useful.

By studying an activity it should be possible to identify not only the key characteristics of the task to be done but also the attributes of the person best suited to perform a particular job or a group of related activities. For example, a site manager may well require a certain level of organisational ability but no exceptional physical strength, whereas a labourer who is regularly involved in heavy lifting does require a good level of physical fitness to perform such duties.

It would be impractical to examine every organisational activity on a regular basis, what is needed is the ability to examine particular activities in an analytical fashion as the need arises.

Once the objectives of either a single activity or group of activities have been established, the next step is to study the levels of the following attributes required by the personnel to be selected:

- Skill – two aspects can be identified here. Analytical skill can be measured to some degree by the qualifications a person has, or by psychological testing carried out by a specialist [11]. Practical skill has normally been gained through a recognised training programme and possibly enhanced by experience. Measurement is probably better defined here than for analytical attributes. It is also a simpler exercise to design training programmes for practical skill acquisition rather than for analytical skills.

- Mental effort – this is allied to a person's analytical abilities and level of intelligence. Qualifications and psychological testing offer guidance here.
- Physical effort – this can be measured in terms of a person's physical fitness and medical record. The effort required to perform a particular activity can be related to a fitness level and regularly monitored to ensure a person's health and safety during employment.
- Responsibility – this will apply in two directions. To whom will a person be responsible and who will be responsible to that person? For example, the site manager will be responsible to the contracts manager; the section foreman will be responsible to the site manager. It is difficult to measure how well responsibilities are being discharged and this tends to be a rather retrospective measurement.
- Working conditions – this is more about the environment that a person will be expected to work in than the individual. Working conditions should clearly reflect the safe performance of activities and the health and well-being of personnel. Consideration should not only be given to physical but also to mental well-being.

To identify activity objectives and then to evaluate activities so that personnel can be deployed efficiently, the examination technique developed by work study practitioners can be employed. To demonstrate how such a questioning technique might be used, an example using the case study company is given in Table 3.1.

The company has decided to employ a senior quantity surveyor and sees this as an opportunity to review its surveying needs. The person employed will have to develop any new surveying and cost control systems that the company concludes are necessary.

This type of analysis can be used in as much detail as a company sees fit, and it is from such an analysis that a job specification for the new quantity surveyor can be produced. The exact structure of the analysis is not important. What is important is the thinking process which identifies the organisational, administrative and management needs of the company when it comes to consider its particular trading situation.

The company can now go on to consider the production of a job specification/job description. It is via the use of such a specification that the company can attempt to find the 'right' person to fill a position with the minimum possibility of mistake. Mistakes do obviously occur in that either the person selected did not really understand what was required, or did not fulfil the expectations of the company. It is via a

Table 3.1   Examination of Quantity Surveying Function and Activities

Questions	Responses	Reasoning
What has to be done?	The administration and management of value and cost on contracts. The design of systems which enable the above to be carried out effectively is also important.	The management accountancy function is normally carried by a quantity surveyor who has been trained in such matters. Without good financial feedback from projects management, decision-making is impaired.
Why does it need to be done?	At present the company uses surveying consultants reporting to the company secretary who then reports on financial matters to the board. There is a feeling that the company secretary has too much work but does not have the required applied training and experience to continue managing the function if the company is to grow. The board requires timely contract accounting data in order to take decisions about present and future workloads.	It is important for any building company to be able to measure profit or loss on contracts effectively. This function requires applied expertise and if carried out inappropriately could prove dangerous.
Who does it and why that person?	The company secretary has a good grounding in financial management theory and practice, and was the obvious person to set up and administer the company's management accounting procedures.	The company could send the company secretary on a training programme. However it was decided that the employment of a trained quantity surveyor would benefit the company in the long term.

continued on page 26

Table 3.1 *continued*

Questions	Responses	Reasoning
Where is it done?	Mainly office based, but sites must be visited regularly.	Contract data must be collected and employed in both valuation and reconciliation systems.
How is it done and how should it be done?	At present consultants produce valuations and agree these with clients' representatives. They then produce cost/value reconciliations only when asked to do so by the company secretary. The board feels that information should be systematically produced at regular intervals.	It is considered desirable to get the quantity surveyor to design and implement a new management accounting system. In this way the new quantity surveyor will have to evaluate and get to know the company's existing systems.
When does it need to be done and why then?	At present the only regularised system is the company's financial accounts. These are produced on a quarterly, half-yearly and yearly basis. The board feels that it would be beneficial to have a management accounting system which allows reports to be produced on a monthly basis.	A regularised management accounting system is highly desirable. If the reporting times can be lined up, data can become more useful.

Table 3.2 Job Specification

(1)	Job title	Senior Quantity Surveyor.
(2)	Job description	The person selected will be required to design and implement a full range of quantity surveying services to suit the company's needs. An ability to analyse company needs and to design systems to suit these needs will be an important attribute. The two key areas that require attention are the production of measured valuations on contracts and subsequent reconciliation of cost with value.
(3)	Responsibility	The person selected will be required to work on his or her own initiative, although he or she will be directly responsible and report to the company secretary. The quantity surveyor may well see the need to recruit suitable additional staff and this exercise will be coordinated by the surveyor and the company secretary.
(4)	Environment	While the quantity surveyor will be based at head office, a reasonable amount of travelling to sites within a 30 mile radius will be required.
(5)	Qualifications and experience	The successful person will be a corporate member of either the CIOB or RICS, and will have at least 10 years' experience working for a construction company, the last 5 being at a senior level.
(6)	Promotional opportunities	It is expected that within a short period of time the successful person will join the board as finance director. Every opportunity will be given to attend training courses and seminars to aid the transition process.
(7)	Employment package	The salary will be commensurate with such a senior position and will be topped up via the company's profit sharing scheme. A non-contributary pension scheme will also apply, as will private health insurance. A company car of a good standard also forms part of the package.

systematic approach that mistakes or errors of judgement are mini-mised. The job specification does not merely act as a selection guide but should also prove useful in identifying the training needs of suc-cessful applicants (the perfect 'fit' does not exist, people generally grow into a job or a role). It should also form the basis against which a person's subsequent performance can be measured. An example of a job specification for the company's new quantity surveyor is shown in Table 3.2 to give an indication of how a typical job specification can be presented.

This type of approach to the production of job specifications can be expanded upon or simplified to suit specific selection or company requirements. The important aspect is that it forms the basis of a structured thinking process which if followed sensibly helps not merely with selection but also has a part to play in evaluating functional needs.

Having specified what is to be done and established the rewards for a particular job, the next step is to examine the attributes that a successful candidate should have in order to perform the activities required. The aim is to select the 'right' person to a job or situation, and for this person to grow and take control of the relevant activities. A useful approach to help the directors of the case study company evaluate the make-up of the person best suited to fill a particular position is to produce a personnel specification.

Over the years there have been many psychological tests developed to measure attributes related to job suitability and performance. However if the results of these tests are to carry any degree of confi-dence, the tests themselves should be done by trained psychologists. What the directors are looking for is again a structure to aid their thinking process and then some criteria upon which to base their selection decisions.

In 1951 the National Institute of Industrial Psychology published a system for 'worker' selection known as the 'Seven Point Plan' [12]. There are two aspects to the use of this plan. The first is in the selection of people for jobs and the second is as a means of giving vocational guidance, i.e. deciding what jobs suit people with a given make-up. It would be useful if the directors were to consider both aspects in their deliberations. Another key point to bear in mind is that selection of people and matching of personnel to jobs should be a continuing process, and that the measurement systems used should not be merely front-end exercises but form part of a reflective system that attempts to evaluate performance.

The seven categories which form the basis of the plan are:

• *Physical make-up* – this covers matters such as health and in particu-lar any disabilities which would mitigate against the employment of a particular person. Also of interest are judgements about a person's appearance and bearing, and communication abilities. In this case, the quantity surveyor will need to be reasonably fit and mobile, of 'smart' appearance, confident and have a high level of communication skills.

- *Attainments* – such matters as educational and occupational training and experience are examined. The quantity surveyor in this case is required to have had a good general education, probably to 'A' level standard, and then to have acquired the professional qualifications set out in the job specification. As identified in the job specification, at least 10 years' experience with at least 5 years in a senior position are essential in this case.
- *General intelligence* – an idea of a person's level of intelligence and how this might be applied will be assessed here. Quite often it is a good idea not merely to accept a person's qualifications as a measure of intelligence but also to ask questions (at the interview) or use a psychological test to verify any impressions gained.
- *Special aptitudes* – mechanical ability, facility with words or a special talent are reviewed here. In the case of the quantity surveyor an ability to organise and design administrative systems is required. The individual will also be required to be highly self-motivated.
- *Interests* – intellectual, conceptual, constructional, physical, social and artistic are all aspects to be identified here. Clearly anybody being considered for a senior management position will need to have a reasonably high intellectual capacity, be able to conceptualise and to have interests outside the work environment.
- *Disposition* – factors to be assessed include dependability, self-reliance, ability to influence others and acceptability to other people. In our case, high levels of all these will need to be demonstrated by candidates.
- *Circumstances* – social background, and domestic circumstances are evaluated here. It will be important for the candidate to live reasonably close to the head office, to have a sound domestic environment and to be reasonably gregarious.

Having identified the functional needs via an examination technique, defined the job via a job specification, and evaluated the make-up of the person most suited to fit needs using a personnel specification, the company should now be in a position to take the next step in the selection process – that of interviewing prospective candidates.

Interviewing

The interviewer (there may well be more than one) must consider the objectives that are to be achieved by the interview process. It is a good idea to produce an interview checklist and a set of initial questions both as a means of clarifying the selection criteria and objectives and as an aid to reflecting upon the behaviour and responses of each interviewee. Clearly, a great deal of subjectivity inevitably forms part of judgements made at and subsequent to the interview, and the idea of using a checklist and initial questions is a means of bringing some structure to the process. The interviewers should try to become familiar with a candidate's biographical details and set these against information given by the candidate in the application and if requested (depending on the nature of the job under consideration) the *curriculum vitae*. It is from both these documents that the initial questions of the interviewer(s) will be developed. It is important for the interviewer(s) to create an air of unobtrusive informality, thus gaining the confidence of the interviewee, while still exercising a degree of control over the proceedings. In order to achieve successful outcomes from interviews it is essential that interviewers are clear about what they are trying to achieve and are skilled in interviewing techniques. Some of the skills can be acquired via education and training and then developed through experience. However, there are certain personal attributes which a good interviewer must have, and which cannot be acquired by study or application. Interviewers should be well adjusted (balanced, and of sound judgement), have an understanding of themselves and be able to project a warm and sincere attitude towards interviewees.

The interviewer will also be trying to gauge personality traits in the candidate and assess the social skills displayed.

It is important to remember that interviews are two-way in nature. The prospective employer is attempting to gain information about a candidate and candidates should also gain information about the organisation they might be joining. The candidate should be encouraged to ask questions at appropriate points during the interview, and it should not be forgotten that candidates will inevitably form opinions about the job and the organisation as a result of the way the interview is conducted. For example, an interview which is conducted in a haphazard fashion without two-way interaction cannot fail to create a poor opinion in the mind of the interviewee.

Some form of assessment or rating system should be employed, taking care to ensure that this is not too mechanistic.

Finally it is essential that all the managers/supervisors associated with the position to be filled have not only been consulted at the preselection phase but are also involved at the selection stage. They should feel that they have all made an input to the process.

Having made a selection based upon a broad review of the criteria collected from the candidate's application statements, *curriculum vitae* (if applicable) and interview performance, the company must now make an offer to the prospective employee and this starts the engagement process.

Engagement

This is a very important aspect when considering the initial and continuing relationship between the company and employee. First impressions can last for a long time and it is important to start off on the correct footing.

It is important that all the relevant paperwork (Contract of Employment, Record of Engagement, Personal Record Card) is completed and ready for checking by both employee and employer on the commencement date. This is not merely a bureaucratic nicety but conveys an air of efficiency which clearly should be aimed for in all company activities.

The offers and agreements made at the interview and offer stages should be ratified and any misunderstandings cleared up to everybody's satisfaction. It is surprising how often the details of an offer, for instance, the salary, is either changed by the prospective employer prior to acceptance or misunderstood by the candidate. These situations can lead to an element of mistrust creeping into the initial relationship, which should be avoided at all costs.

No matter what level a new recruit enters, a personal record card is a useful tool in detailing and measuring an individual's existing and developing characteristics. Information kept in such a recording system should ideally be the subject of discussions between employer and employee at regular intervals.

The objective of this chapter has not been to examine the recruitment function in great detail, since there are many good texts which seek to do this, but rather to relate people to jobs or functions in a systematic fashion. Prior to moving on to the measurement of performance, reference will be made to the induction process and to career development.

Induction

The taking up of a position with a new company and new people is quite stressful to any individual. Induction should therefore be a gradual process whereby information is imparted at a sensible pace, not overburdening and confusing the new recruit. The induction process seeks to introduce and inform the employee about the company, the job and the general employment conditions.

A useful approach to convey such information is to produce a company handbook. This is a more meaningful way to present details of the company's background, aims and past achievements than would be achieved by verbal communication. The company's organisation (perhaps using charts) with, if possible, biographical details of key management figures can also be presented to good effect in the handbook. However, care should be taken to ensure that the information given is as up-to-date as possible, since outdated information can be the source of problems from a number of standpoints. Other matters which are also usefully conveyed in writing are the general objectives and policies of the company, and any organised social activities which occur regularly.

The handbook does not take the place of the very important personal introduction procedure whereby new employees are shown around the organisation, introduced formally to the people they are going to work with and actually shown the facilities at their disposal. There is no alternative to this aspect of induction.

Induction should not be seen as just an initial exercise. It makes sense to check, at appropriate intervals, that new recruits are settling in and experiencing no major problems.

Career development

Consideration of each employee's career development is a sound thing to do from the company's viewpoint. People are a company's most important assets, and improvements in an individual's abilities should be seen as a sensible investment in a company's future.

The company should seek to establish a partnership with each of its employees, in order to agree a development path which is flexible and meets the needs of both company and employee.

The next aspect with which the company should concern itself is to measure performance with a view to maintaining or improving manpower efficiency. The use of the word 'manpower' applies to both managerial and operational personnel, and an important aspect in both cases is the individuals' ability to recognise whether they are working to the best of their abilities or whether improvements can be made.

When the concept of performance measurement is mentioned there is a danger that it is viewed at a purely mechanistic level whereby 'inputs' (effort, resources) are compared with 'outputs' (products) and a statement about productivity and efficiency is made in respect of a particular task or groups of activities. There is a need to measure and compare at this level so long as any comparisons made are in context and all the constraints which apply to a particular process at any particular time are taken into account. For example, it would be unfair to compare two operatives carrying out the same task, after one has been trained to use a specific power tool to speed up the work while the other is still doing the job manually. The same applies to training and abilities for particular tasks or functions. An attempt must be made to compare like with like in order to make intelligent judgements about where improvements can be made both to the individual's attributes via education/training and to the acquisition and development of aids to improve the way in which jobs are carried out. What is needed is a broad view of performance/efficiency when examining people and their jobs. As stated above, if individuals can be encouraged to take control of their own work situation and to identify for themselves where improvements can be made, they will feel more motivated to make these changes in practice and to get involved with their own 'growth' process in the work environment. If this type of ethos can be fostered in an organisation at all levels there can be substantial gains from the management's standpoint as well as the individual's. This type of philosophy leads to what are often termed *people development programmes*.

People development programmes

For these programmes to work effectively a partnership must exist between a manager and the person responsible to him. This is important at all levels within an organisation. Take, for example, the experienced middle-aged supervisor who is rather set in his ways. If this man is told he is to be sent off on a training programme with little or no consultation, the result at best will be begrudged attendance with possible psychological barriers to learning having been set up. At worst there may well be outright conflict between manager and supervisor. An important aspect of the situation identified here is one of perception and understanding. The manager needs to understand the ways in which the supervisor might perceive the reasons for the organisation wanting to send him on such an exercise. The manager should have identified a need for training (considered when discussing manpower planning) and clarified the nature and type of training required prior to attempting implementation. The supervisor should be aware of this process and be encouraged to see the benefits not just from a company standpoint but also from his own. Quite often in situations such as this an individual can feel threatened, and this must be avoided or at the very least understood and taken account of.

There are therefore two aspects to people development programmes. The first is the identification of a need to change or improve the way things are done. A company's senior managers should be continually reviewing company performance on a broad basis and identifying the abilities and skills needed to improve it. The second is to agree how, when and what type of personal development are required. It is the second aspect which is considered here, the first being discussed later under the concept of manpower planning. In order to relate the organisation's needs with an individual's aspirations and own set of objectives, the principles of the theory of management by objectives (MBO) is a useful vehicle. As with the other techniques and theories described, it is not the intention to suggest that they are either followed rigidly or applied without question. The objective is to present a structure within which the important decision-making process can take place.

The underlying theme of MBO is that of trying to clarify the objectives and goals of managers and to see that the responsibility for attaining these goals is reasonably distributed throughout a management team. In order to do this a set of objective standards of performance against which management behaviour can be measured must be agreed. It is also important to encourage managers to play a creative part in establishing such standards, and to ensure this is being done. The first step in the exercise will be the establishment of the main objectives of the organisation. These main objectives are then broken down into a series of sub-objectives at each of the operational levels of the organisation so that managers can clarify the sub-goals which need to be achieved in order that overall organisational goals are ultimately met.

Humble [13,14] suggests that improving business results is a continuous process. Managers should examine, measure and compare information from the strategic plan, devolving it into tactical plans and then down to the operational planning level. Managers should attempt to compare actual results with planned results, and feed this information back up to the strategic level. In this way a series of realistic objectives can be set at each level in an organisation. Hence managers can evaluate progress towards attaining their goals or more importantly identify obstacles in the way of achievement of these objectives.

The key benefits of employing this approach are:

- Managers are encouraged to contribute to the setting of clearly understood performance standards, and from this it can be argued that they will show enhanced commitment to the achievement of these targets.
- Managers should also show a commitment to the production of their own control data, which also becomes more meaningful throughout the feedback system.
- The performance of managers can be systematically reviewed and education/training plans for management development can be drawn up and reviewed in the light of the dynamics of the business environment.

- It can also be argued that managers' motivation may well be reinforced by a closer involvement with the development of their own future prospects.

Humble also regards management development as a by-product of business efficiency, and therefore the development of the business should go hand in hand with the growth and development of managers.

If MBO is seen in its broadest form, a system for a people development programme can be set up to cater for everybody in the organisation and not merely for personnel considered to be management. The system in its simplest form attempts to match the organisation's needs with the needs and aspirations of the people that go to make up the organisation – from the managing director, who may well have a clear idea of where he is going and what he wants from life, to the young new site trainee, who might well not have such a clear idea of either.

While the approach adopted when considering a programme for management development will be different in emphasis from one that would be used for trainees, however the underlying principles are the same. What one is trying to achieve, with a carefully considered programme, is the blending of educational/training to the needs of the job and the development of the individual.

From an administrative standpoint the development programme can form part of the information recorded within a 'personal record' system. In order to describe how such a programme can be operated it is useful to take the example of a manager/subordinate relationship. Prior to an initial interview, the manager establishes a series of objectives and goals considered appropriate for the subordinate in question. This should not be seen as a means of forcing these objectives upon a person, but rather of attempting to structure a dialogue and as a first step in a negotiating process. The initial interview should be seen as a means of discussing company objectives and company expectations and linking these with those of the subordinate. Negotiation should then follow whereby agreed objectives and goals which are seen to be achievable over an agreed time scale are set down. This initial interview is the foundation for regular review discussions which seek to monitor progress and to vary the programme to suit both individual and company needs. It must not be forgotten that such programmes should be flexible, to take account of the individual's speed of learning or capacity to acquire new abilities.

The two main aspects to be considered and taken account of within any programme are:

- Education/training.
- Guided experience.

These aspects will be emphasised differently for different people. Education/training provision may be supplied in a variety of ways, either using external courses produced and delivered by education establishments or training organisations, or by in-house delivered exercises. The main problem associated with external courses is that of continuity of quality and subject matter. It is therefore sensible to build up a relationship with an external provider and to keep courses under constant review.

An advantage of external training courses is that it enables individuals to mix with people from other organisations, thus allowing interchanges of ideas and the stimulation of new ideas, which not only has benefits for individuals/companies but also for the industry as a whole.

The notion of guided experience applies to all the learning situations that individuals find themselves in, throughout any organisation. This is a central theme in the MBO approach to development programmes. In the management context, junior managers gradually assume responsibility under the guidance of a senior manager so ensuring that suitable performance checks are made from time to time. This idea of experiential learning formed the basis of apprenticeship schemes, which in recent years have diminished following arguments about whether they are flexible enough to train people in rapidly changing business environments, and also because of recessions in the construction industry. The modern view is that people need to train rapidly and learn new skills in line with changes in work practices brought about by technological and economic developments. There is however a danger in taking such a stance – that of viewing skills/abilities as simply being acquired and very easily changed. Careful consideration must be given to the foundations required before skills and abilities can be developed. There has been a move towards the over-simplification of operational practices in recent years and from this, of management applications in the construction industry. This has been instrumental in de-skilling the industry's workforce. The notion that skills and abilities are easily acquired and interchangeable should be carefully considered. It is too early to evaluate the damage that may well have been done in applying such attitudes to training and education. This will only become apparent in the early part of the next century.

Measurement of performance

If companies are serious about developing people's skills then it is essential that each individual's performance is regularly reviewed. There are two clear objectives for carrying out performance appraisal exercises, and it is important that both reviewer and reviewee are clear as to what is to be achieved. The first objective is an attempt to encourage the people under review to evaluate their own performance against a set of agreed short-term objectives. The reviewer should be prepared to encourage an open dialogue which clearly identifies perceived areas where more effort or improvements need to be made. Emphasis should be placed upon aspects of an individual's work which have been particularly good, so that the motivational aspect of deserved praise comes into play. The second objective is linked to a company's reward and remuneration system. It is vital that people can see a clear ladder of opportunity within any organisation. They need to feel that if they perform to the best of their ability and demonstrate both acumen and potential in given circumstances then they will be rewarded in two ways. First that they will be given greater opportunities to take on more responsibility and perhaps more demanding tasks, and second that they will be rewarded financially within a company's clearly defined remuneration system.

It is dangerous to attempt to link these two objectives too closely. Take for example a manager who is working on a particularly difficult contract, and because of circumstances beyond his control does not achieved agreed objectives. It would be unfair not to take on board circumstances which impede or constrain people's ability to perform as well as they might given their capacity at any given stage in their careers. Having said this, it is essential to ensure that too much subjectivity does not unduly influence the judgements arrived at by the person carrying out the review process, although this is very difficult to assess.

To help ensure that the two objectives, personal development and reward, are not confused in the review system it is a good idea to keep them separate during the review processes. This is not to say that they cannot be assessed at the same time. For example, although assessments of an individual's performance and potential are being made as part of the day-to-day relationship of superior to subordinate, it is important to formalise such evaluations within regular review interviews. It is at these interviews that the subjectivity arising out of reflecting upon the way a person reacts or fails to react under the pressure of the work situation can be rationalised. An aid to this process is to set out what is to be achieved as a result of the interview. The interviewee should be left in no doubt as to the outcomes of the review process and should not be in a position to feel aggrieved if rewards are not forthcoming because desired performance levels or responsibilities have not been achieved. For this to occur, people must know what is required of them and from this knowledge be able to make judgements as to how well they are conforming to such requirements. At each stage of an individual's development it must be clear how new levels of responsibility or more demanding tasks can be achieved. Clearly subjectivity cannot be eliminated from the judgement process, however it can be minimised by employing a structured approach to measuring performance. The management by objectives philosophy requires that performance objectives are agreed, and therefore it makes sense that agreement is sought that they have been achieved and at what level. Having reached agreement in respect of performance and desired outcomes, rewards in whatever form chosen should be forthcoming. There is nothing more damaging to morale than to have performed to an agreed or better than agreed standard and then not to be rewarded in the way expected.

The link between performance and cost

In chapter 1 reference was made to the problem of acquiring suitable labour in line with the need to maintain desired quality on contracts. It was also noted that this also posed a problem for supervision in that if quality levels are to be maintained, either higher levels (in terms of number of workers) or better quality supervision (if labour quality is declining) will be required. The question of whether the quality of the labour available in the construction industry is or has been declining in recent times has been the subject of debate, and will continue to be so for the foreseeable future. What is of concern here is that the case study company is facing a problem of recruiting suitable labour and therefore must develop strategies to deal or cope with the situation. Either the work carried out should be kept in line with the skills and abilities of the workforce available (i.e. carrying out work which is not perceived to be or not needed to be of a high quality) or the company will need to pay a premium to attract more highly skilled workers. There is a cost penalty to both situations, although in practice this is difficult to identify or measure. This being the case, a more reflective approach to any judgements arrived at is needed. Most companies are not in a position to select and control the markets they operate in. An honest appraisal of the people employed should be attempted. In line with this appraisal will be the need to budget for any 'quality control' measures considered necessary, not forgetting that in competitive markets allowances such as these may well be counterproductive. The important thing to bear in mind is the need to measure the effects of attaining desired quality, whether laid down by clients or expected by the company. These effects can inhibit a company's overall financial performance and needs to be considered within a cost monitoring and control system.

Summary

The objective of this chapter was to examine how personnel can be employed and then deployed to suit objectives laid down by a manpower plan. The production of this manpower plan was not discussed here but the aim was rather to review the relationships to be considered between jobs to be performed and the people who perform them.

The first step is to analyse an activity in a structured way so that the key aspects are identified. Criteria such as skill, mental/physical effort, responsibility and working conditions are identified in order that the parameters within which activities are performed can be specified. An examination technique can then be used to evaluate what is required from a function and how it might be carried out.

The next step is to produce a job specification which defines the job, thus enabling the characteristics of the person needed to carry out the job to be assessed. As an aid to identifying the attributes desired in a person for a particular role, the notion of using a personnel specification was identified.

The information produced in the job specification and the personnel specification can then be evaluated and set against the people selected for interview. It is imperative that interviews are conducted in a structured fashion and that interviewers are working to a clear set of objectives. It is also useful to employ some form of rating system, always ensuring that it is not too mechanistic.

Having selected an appropriate person and received confirmation that this individual is willing to join the company, a formal engagement procedure should be initiated. It is emphasised that engagement procedures should not be seen as mere paperwork exercises, because it is important at this stage to get off on the right foot and to ensure that both parties are happy with the agreements made and the packages offered.

An important aspect of introducing new people to organisations is induction. The aim here is not only to introduce them to the people and systems they will be working with, but also to ensure they feel increasingly part of the organisation. A useful tool to aid this process is the development and use of a company handbook.

It is very important that people are encouraged to fulfil their own career and personal objectives. The idea of employing people development programmes for all company employees is put forward as a means of fostering such a philosophy, and central to such schemes is the use of some form of management by objectives.

The final two sections of the chapter deal with the measurement of performance and the link between performance and cost. There seems little point in setting up a process of agreeing objectives with people and then not bothering to measure achievement. Performance measurement should be seen as a partnership, and perhaps the best possible form of motivational force is the self-motivational one, whereby self-improvement comes about because opportunities are available for people to take control of their own performance at whatever level they are operating at within an organisation.

4 Materials Management

Introduction

If one considers the relative value (i.e. materials value to total contract value) of the materials that are required to be purchased and used for any contract, it can easily be appreciated how important are the materials management functions.

Two distinct but highly related processes or groups of processes are required to be performed in the acquiring and using of materials on sites:

- Procurement.
- Management from supply to incorporation.

This chapter seeks to examine the processes required for the efficient acquisition and use of materials at the 'right' time, to an 'acceptable' price/cost and most importantly to a desired quality level. Associated with these aims will be a company's ability to reconcile the materials actually used on contracts with those planned to be used.

Procurement objectives

Before reviewing a company's procurement objectives it is useful to consider when the procurement process actually starts. In effect it really starts with the decisions made by the designer in selecting the materials and technology, and the quality levels dictated by someone's 'value' criteria. However our case study company will only get involved with such judgements and decision-making in its speculative work. It is perhaps easier to manage the procurement process when one is involved with design decision-making. Generally when companies are operating in the contracting sphere of the industry their input into design aspects is limited by the contractual arrangements under which the work is tendered for and carried out.

For the purpose of this chapter the process of materials procurement commences at the tender stage, after a designer has selected and produced a design and the project is ready to be put out to tender. The reason for selecting this as the starting point is that the cost/price decisions taken by the estimator, and subsequently included within a tender, become the budget reference points against which 'gains/ losses' are measured. The material cost/price element of a tender becomes the material budget on a 'live' contract. This being the case, it is very important that due consideration is given to quoting levels of cost/price within tenders that are at least those which allow materials to be acquired. There is therefore a need for estimators to keep abreast of market conditions: either they are provided with information by a company's buying department (the buying function is managed by one of the case study company's working directors) or they must themselves acquire current market data and use this appropriately.

The key procurement objective of any company is the provision of the 'right' materials at the 'right' time, in the 'right' place and to an agreed budget such that progress on sites is uninterrupted. Underlying this key objective are sub-objectives or things that need to be achieved to ensure that the key objective is met more often than not.

The following are some of the more important matters that need to be addressed:

- Investigation, locating, selecting and fostering relationships with suppliers. There is a need to seek possible new suppliers for a number of reasons, such as changes in market circumstances. Relationships with key people in a supply organisation are important in order that the best possible terms and conditions are obtained and also to ensure efficient management of the actual supply and delivery of materials.
- It is important to adopt a systematic approach to obtaining quotations from the 'best' sources. An ability to judge competitiveness and to negotiate where appropriate is something to aim for, and systemisation is an aid to this aim.
- Materials need to be taken off (using contract documentation) and collected in a way that fulfils the needs of the key objective. Materials schedules (see Figure 4.4) are useful tools in this respect.
- There is a need to keep abreast of what is happening in markets for a number of reasons. New materials and ways of using materials may well have productivity benefits attached. Costs/prices can fall as well as rise in the short term, and it is the companies who can take advantage of market circumstances that gain over their competitors.

- Records of the company's dealings with suppliers should be kept if the notions of feedback and learning about successes and failures are to be followed.
- The maintenance of an adequate relationship with sites is very important. The status of orders placed and deliveries required, and the measurement of how well a supplier is meeting company and site needs, must be evaluated. ᵗ

It is now appropriate to consider how purchasing can take place in a building context such that a company's cost and time considerations are facilitated.

The nature of purchasing

It has often been stated by various writers that a contractor has to set up a 'factory' afresh every time a contract is won. Construction projects, while encompassing numerous building processes, are nevertheless different from normal factory production which is characterised by continuous repetitive processes. Continuous repetitive processes lend themselves to planning for forward purchasing and often allow the advantages of bulk purchasing to be obtained. If such approaches are adopted in the construction environment, a considerable amount of care is required. The nature of construction markets generally mitigates against the acquisition and stockpiling of large quantities of materials unless they are for speculative areas of work and even here, because of the need to comply with differing planning and design requirements, benefits tend to be marginalised. Another factor to bear in mind here is the need for large storage areas and the cost of administering storage. In any case, with such a large national network of material and component suppliers, contractors need to identify and plan their resource needs on a contract-by-contract basis, unless an alternative arrangement can be proved to have a time, organisational or cost benefit.

Purchasing methods

There are three basic approaches which can be adopted:

(1) All purchasing is dealt with by site personnel under the control of the site manager and within guidelines set out by a contracts manager. This approach is predominantly used by the case study company and is only really suitable on small contracts or very large jobs. On a very large project the site manager will be technically responsible but would normally have the on-site services of a

buyer. The major problem with this approach is the coordination and administration of supplies across all the company's jobs within the original objectives identified earlier. Given this approach it may be impossible to negotiate the 'best' price and ensure that payments are made at the correct level and on time to achieve discounts.

(2) A general buyer is employed who is responsible for the purchasing of materials for jobs and for the needs of the company as a whole. In larger companies, buyers are responsible for geographical areas or groups of contracts. In this case buyers may not be able to specialise in particular types of materials (or in fact sub-contracts – see chapter 6 for discussion of sub-contract procurement) but they may be able to build up expertise in respect of work types, e.g. building, civil engineering, private housing, etc.

(3) In the larger organisations and if one takes on board that it is beneficial to build up a specialist knowledge of particular resources and with this foster a relationship with particular suppliers, buyers are encouraged to specialise in groups of resources and or project types. It is their responsibility to gain and maintain a knowledge of sources and trends in their speciality. Of course there is a danger that buyers in particular areas may become redundant with the passing of time and technological advances. However, part of building up expertise is gaining insights into new developments and from this the understanding of when change or development of new expertise is required.

It is considered that the actual method or methods adopted are unimportant, compared with the efficient maintenance of the purchasing function in line with the objectives previously listed (see the section on Purchasing objectives). In order for this to occur, one person within the organisation should have the responsibility of overseeing and organising the buying function. Smaller companies appear to fall down in this respect, tending to follow a rather *laissez faire* approach with method (1) predominating. This results in:

- Over-ordering of materials, with associated wastage problems.
- Over-payment for materials because of inadequate administration procedures.
- Loss of benefits from the lack of skilled negotiating procedures which would accrue from the employment of purchasing expertise.
- Lack of knowledge as to when and where the best service/source might be available at any particular time.

Methods (2) and (3) may well not be cost effective for very small companies. However as a company grows in terms of turnover and hence financial resources, these are the approaches likely to produce the best results. Nevertheless it is vital even for the smallest company to adopt a structured approach to purchasing, against a clear set of guidelines.

Centralised versus decentralised purchasing

As with the basic methods of purchasing there are three basic alternatives with regard to the form of buying organisation and its position within the framework of a company as a whole. To a large extent the choice will depend on the nature of the company and the type of work it carries out. The three alternatives are:

- A centralised approach whereby all purchasing is organised and carried out by one person or within one department. This means that no matter what the nature of an item (from a paper clip to curtain walling) or the quantity needed, the actual purchase will be carried out by the central purchasing source.
- A decentralised approach whereby sites, departments or areas are responsible for their own purchasing needs.
- A centralised/decentralised approach which seeks to attract the benefits associated with the individual approaches.

Each department or section of an organisation will need to purchase a broad range of items while carrying out construction work and in the general running of the business. Management and administration of the business will require office equipment, stationery and other communication equipment. During a construction project there will be a need both to buy the raw materials and components of building and also to buy or hire plant and equipment to aid the various construction processes. Experience shows that the best approach, provided the company can afford to ('afford' in its broadest sense), is to adopt a centralised/decentralised system. This means that all major items are purchased centrally by one source. However, localised or departmentalised purchasing is also allowed in order to take account of local circumstances, but within a framework and guidelines set out by the person responsible for the overall buying function. The benefits derived from operating this type of system are:

- Bulk purchasing can be organised by a central department, and hence sites/offices receive coordinated deliveries.
- Bulk purchasing, if carried out efficiently, can lead to substantial discounts.

- Knowledgeable specialists or even local buyers might be able to obtain favourable local terms.
- Large user discounts can be negotiated based on the level of purchasing over a trading period.
- Although it prevents the uncontrolled purchasing of many different uncoordinated 'buyers', it does not mitigate against local purchasing when this course is more sensible. An important point here is that it allows initiative to be shown.

Elements of purchasing

In line with a company's procurement objectives, the three elements that must be identified in any purchasing situation are:

- Quality.
- Price/cost.
- Delivery (time factor).

The importance of each element can be appreciated by considering the following situation: although the cost of a particular material is comparatively low, the prospect of a reasonable delivery time is remote. In this case the choice of a more expensive source to achieve the target delivery might be the sensible option.

The task of getting all three elements at a desired level on any contract for any one material is often difficult to achieve. Each element is now considered separately.

(1) Quality

This is the key element and might only be achievable at the expense of the other two.

In the construction industry the required quality of materials and components will be laid down to a large extent in the contract documents, i.e. specifications, drawings and possibly a bill of quantities. Nevertheless there should still be scope for a keen buyer to probe the market for the cheapest price within a quality range, or suggest alternative materials and components which are of equivalent quality.

(2) Price

Price is to a large extent governed by the law of supply and demand, although the more modern concept of 'what the market will bear' will also apply to those suppliers seeking the best possible price without losing custom.

In the construction industry, cycles of construction activity have a considerable effect on materials markets. It therefore follows that manufacturers and suppliers with empty order books will give lower quotations until the markets improve.

How then are prices obtained? A typical approach might be as follows:

- Select the suppliers to receive requests for quotations. This selection is normally on the basis of previous experience. It is a good idea to maintain some reference system which gives a quick and convenient record of a company's dealings with individual suppliers.
- Send out enquiries. These enquiries should give all relevant information to assist the supplier in submitting a price:
  1. Quantity required.
  2. Specification and full description of material or component.
  3. Where delivery is to be made.
  4. Timing of delivery.
  5. Idea of when a firm order may be placed.
- Receipt and analysis of quotes. It is a good idea to tabulate the quotations to aid comparison, and these tabulations form useful reference material for live and future contracts. Figure 4.1 is an example of a comparison pro-forma. Such pro-formas can be used as a classification system for suppliers by type of material or component. A little further analysis can produce a list of suppliers who regularly quote favourably, and the ones who generally do not can be removed from quotation lists.
- Under normal circumstances the cheapest will be chosen. However it must be ensured that:
  1. The supplier is aware of the time factors involved.
  2. All qualifications stipulated by the supplier (if acceptable) were taken into account when comparisons were made.
  3. All quotes are based on the same information.

As mentioned earlier, it is very important that buyers are continually testing the market to ensure that prices being paid are the best available. However, the playing-off of one tenderer against another (Dutch auctions) should not be countenanced, as this not only leads to bad feeling but also to offers being made and accepted which cannot be fulfilled.

Before moving on to discuss delivery, an aspect of 'price' which tends either to be underrated or managed inefficiently – that of discounts – will be mentioned. Discounts are an important source of revenue which in many cases are not fully appreciated at the pre- or post-contract stages of a project. There are three basic forms of discount which can be offered by suppliers:

Quotation Analysis Pro-forma

Supplier/Sub-contractor:					Tender/Contract: Ref.:		
Prepared by:					Date:		

Submitted by:	1	2	3	4	5	6
Date:						
Price:						
Terms & Conditions:						
Unit Price:						
Time Quote valid for:						
Best On-site Delivery Date:						
Consistency of pricing:						
Choice of Supplier or Sub-contractor:						
Reason for Choice:						

Signed by Buyer:	Date:
Signed by Contracts Manager/Director:	Date:
Signed by Surveyor:	Date:

Figure 4.1   Quotation analysis pro-forma

(1) Cash discounts are generally allowed for prompt payment of accounts rendered. The normal allowance is 2½% for making payment within 28 days of receipt of an invoice. This type of discount should not be passed on or allowed for in the main contractor's tender, because if the terms of the allowance are not met then the discount will not be given. This key aspect is often mismanaged by purchasers and suppliers alike. Quite often, and particularly in recessionary periods, contractual payment requirements are

ignored. Payments are made late but the purchaser still deducts and thus benefits from a cash discount. Either suppliers are not monitoring these occurrences efficiently or they are reluctant to complain and rectify the situation, possibly for commercial reasons. The other major aspect of mismanagement in respect of such discounts is the passing on of the expected savings to prospective clients to gain an edge on competitors. Clearly, if cash discounts are not achieved then they can become another factor which reduces expected margins at the post-contract stage of projects.

(2) Trade discounts are normally given to purchasers who buy in large quantities. The size of discount varies with the size of purchase. Over the years this type of discount seems to have been eroded in that a discount is given as an automatic part of a transaction simply because a purchaser is in the trade, thus every purchase carries a discount irrespective of quantity. It is therefore important for buyers to examine the discounts they are achieving critically, to establish if they are achieving a 'true' saving as a result of trading with a particular supplier or merely a discount offered to all purchasers irrespective of trading considerations.

(3) Cumulative discounts are a variation of trade discounts. A calculation of the actual discount is normally made at the end of a trading period, based on the level of total purchases over a period of time.

It is clearly possible to create variants of the above. However the important thing is for speedy negotiations to take place, followed by efficient monitoring to ensure the agreed discounts are adhered to.

(3) Delivery (time factor)

Quotations are normally obtained at the tender stage. The first objective of a buyer is to establish for what period a quote will be valid. Some suppliers will hold a quotation firm for long periods while others will not, depending on economic circumstances and a supplier's judgement of risk.

A two-stage view must be adopted by a buyer. At the tender stage, quotations will reflect the nature of the information provided by the purchaser and the market circumstances for such purchases, with limited allowance made for factors which might affect 'price' and delivery at a future date. Market circumstances can change rapidly and buyers must be aware of this. At the post-contract stage, when a project is running, the following questions should be posed and answered:

• Which quotations are still valid in terms of price and delivery? The answer to this question depends on the decisions made at the tender stage by the buyer or estimator.

- Is there a need for more quotations to be sought? The answer to this question depends on the number of quotations which are no longer valid and whether market circumstances have changed to such an extent that it might now be possible to gain much improved deals from suppliers with empty order books. Clearly there are advantages to be gained from seeking new quotations once contracts have been awarded.

It will be a rare occurrence if all three factors (quality, price, delivery) can be resolved satisfactorily in terms of a company's objectives, for every material on each contract. However it is vital that the quality aspect is achieved, because cost and time will suffer if it is not. Thus the quality factor is the primary purchasing objective while price and delivery factors are only secondary objectives to be achieved in line with profit margin and programme considerations.

It is useful to view a typical purchasing procedure for a company as commencing with the receipt of a tender, running through the award/contract stage, on to completion and finally reconciliation and review of achievement. Figure 4.2 depicts a typical procedure in the form of a flowchart.

Purchase orders

Once a suitable supplier has been selected, the next step in the purchasing process is to raise and issue an order to the supplier which will constitute a legal contract when the supplier (seller) accepts or acknowledges receipt of the order. In effect the order becomes a written commitment to accept and pay for goods under an agreed set of terms and conditions. A typical purchase order should include the following details:

- Reference to the original enquiry.
- Detailed description of the goods.
- Quantity required.
- Price as per quotation.
- Where to deliver the goods.
- Programme of delivery requirements – care is necessary here in that it should be clearly stated that any dates given are for guidance purposes only and that firm delivery dates will be supplied via a schedule which will be confirmed or updated in line with contract requirements. It is also essential to bear in mind that any changes to requirements are not only made within the original framework of the order terms and conditions but are also communicated in reasonable time for them to be actioned.
- Order number.

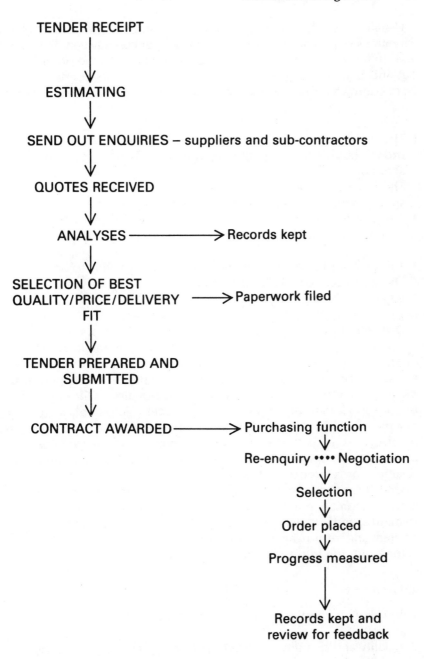

TENDER RECEIPT

↓

ESTIMATING

↓

SEND OUT ENQUIRIES – suppliers and sub-contractors

↓

QUOTES RECEIVED

↓

ANALYSES ──────────→ Records kept

↓

SELECTION OF BEST
QUALITY/PRICE/DELIVERY ──────→ Paperwork filed
FIT

↓

TENDER PREPARED AND
SUBMITTED

↓

CONTRACT AWARDED ───────→ Purchasing function

↓

Re-enquiry •••• Negotiation

↓

Selection

↓

Order placed

↓

Progress measured

↓

Records kept and
review for feedback

Figure 4.2   Typical purchasing procedure

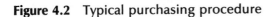

Usually on the back of the order will be printed a brief outline of the conditions of purchase. If there are any differences between 'purchaser' and 'seller' conditions, these must be settled before the order is sent out and becomes a purchase/supply contract. Actual conditions vary from contractor to contractor, but most orders contain clauses which state:

- The purchaser reserves the right to cancel the whole or part of the order should the supplier not comply with the conditions prescribed.
- The quality of the goods supplied must be in accordance with the specification and must be approved by the purchaser.
- The date of delivery/deliveries will be as shown either overleaf or in a schedule provided and any changes to dates can only be by mutual agreement.
- The account to be charged and where the invoice is to be sent.
- The terms and conditions associated with the delivery, e.g. unloading and checking/verification requirements.

Distribution of the purchase order will vary from one company to another, however it is important to ensure that the minimum number of copies are produced and distributed bearing in mind efficient operation and cost effectiveness. Figure 4.3 identifies four copies as the minimum compatible with efficient information flow. One copy is sent to the supplier and sets up the supply process. Another is sent to site as a means of checking the details and progress of the supply process. A third is sent to the accounts department ready for the payment process to be verified and administered, with the final copy being retained for reference by the buyer.

One important aspect of order production and placing is that of authorisation. A purchase order must have a place for the buyer's signature, and it is also good practice to provide space for the supplier to sign and return an acknowledgement that he has received and agrees with the terms and conditions of the order.

Control

Control of purchasing implies that a balance will be achieved between:

- Quality and quantity required by drawings and specifications.
- Quality and quantity of materials ordered.
- Quality and quantity used.
- Sequencing and delivery requirements as planned.
- Sequencing and delivery as achieved.

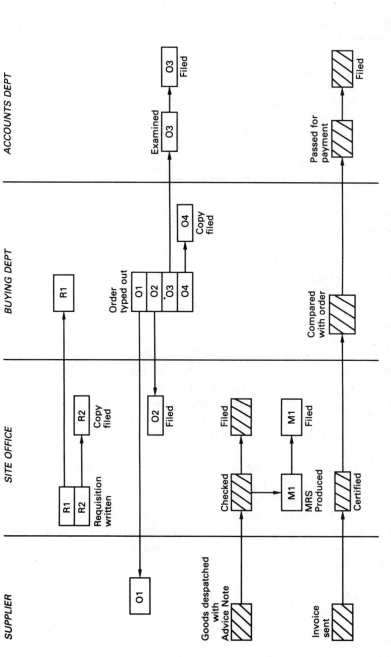

Figure 4.3 Paperwork required in the purchasing system [after Calvert R. E., *Introduction to Building Management*, Butterworth, 1989]

Some form of reconciliation system should be instituted which allows variances from planned materials acquisition and use to be identified and reviewed.

Control in fact must start at the description and take-off stage. It is at this point that quality and quantity are initially identified. Efficient taking-off relies not only on the information supplied by an architect or quantity surveyor, but also on good recording systems. The use of materials schedules which allow not only materials to be described and quantified but also reconciliations and progress reviews to be carried out can help in the overall control process. Figure 4.4 is an example of a materials schedule which attempts to integrate information across the planned and actual usage boundaries. As with all administrative systems, problems will arise and it is worth considering some of these with a view to ensuring that they are minimised.

The most common problems associated with material supply are:

- Taking-off and scheduling – generally materials are either under/over-measured and may also be mis-entered on a schedule. As with most things, care is the remedy and a structured approach should be adopted to measurement and scheduling, with people checking one another's work whenever possible.
- Requisitioning and ordering – the main problem here is normally lack of information on the requisition or order sent to the supplier. Two things need to be considered: (1) to produce pro-forma requisition and order forms which encourage adequate descriptions to be entered; (2) to encourage individuals to fill in the forms to the desired level – this is perhaps the more difficult aspect in that it requires management skill in getting such a message across to individuals.
- Receipt and checking of deliveries from suppliers – this can present major problems on sites. It is vital that when materials are received on site they are fit for their purpose and of the right quantity. In this way progress is maintained and payment problems do not occur. The solution is to install an effective receipt and checking mechanism whereby materials are visually checked via some form of sampling at each delivery. The use of materials received sheets which accurately record the delivery and cross-reference this with the materials schedule and the order should also be encouraged.
- Off-loading and handling – it is essential here that sensible decisions are taken at the tender stage to ensure that adequate equipment is selected and allowed for in the tender. This can then be acquired and used on site. A high proportion of wastage can be attributed to inadequate unloading and handling facilities which in many cases can be traced back to bad tendering decisions.

- Storing and protecting – as with unloading and handling, storage and protection require close attention at the tender stage. Many materials are easily damaged if left unprotected and it makes good sense to store materials so that they are easily retrieved from storage in a ready-for-use condition.
- Issuing and distributing – significant amounts of materials are mislaid and stolen from building sites without anyone being aware of the loss. It is therefore very important that issues of materials are recorded and only available to recognised operatives. Many items, such as ironmongery, are easily removed from site and it clearly makes sense to minimise opportunities for breaches of security.
- Use of materials – this is essentially a production management problem and due consideration should be given to the selection and management of production methods again at the tender stage.
- Quality control and supervision – adequate consideration must be given to the operation of a quality management system. This should define the initial quality of a particular item and then monitor this quality from order to delivery, and to eventual inclusion in the project. A good quality management system should identify problem areas early enough to allow corrective action to be taken.
- Security – this was touched upon earlier. Good site security relies upon making it difficult to remove or damage materials from site. Consideration must be given to the location of the site and the type and nature of materials to be stored on site. Essentially security is a matter of deterrence and should ensure that detection is rapid if theft is occurring or could occur.

The legal aspect of purchasing

If one considers the large amounts of money involved in any company's materials dealings then clearly the legal aspects of purchasing must be borne in mind. It is good practice to engage a lawyer to draft contracts and formulate purchase orders, particularly where they involve complicated clauses such as penalty clauses.

It is clearly advantageous to standardise the approach based on good advice, so that any contracts or orders can be universally and uniformly used for long periods without major revision.

The purchase order is a legal document which gives authority to a supplier to charge for goods as stipulated in the document. It is also the company's commitment to pay for the goods as and when the contract is completed satisfactorily.

The order becomes a legal document when the supplier agrees to transfer the goods to the company for payment. To complete this cycle the supplier must acknowledge receipt of the order, and in most cases a form or slip is attached to the document which has to be completed and returned by the supplier.

Two important points to remember when reviewing purchase orders are:

(1) Only material above the signature is binding.
(2) Alterations to anything on the order must be initialled and clear agreement signified.

It is a good office procedure for all acceptances to be registered on receipt, and in fact to be chased if not received by the due date. It is also very important that the same procedures of notification and acceptance are adopted where variations occur to the original order.

Follow-up procedures

There are two key aspects which should be examined under this heading:

• Progressing.
• Receiving and checking.

Progressing

Production on site depends on the supply of materials and components to the right quality and to a desired programme. If materials are not supplied at the right time then the project will suffer delays and loss of production. The industry is full of optimists who will agree to supply goods at the outset of a contract and for many reasons be unable to deliver these goods on time. It is therefore important to adopt a system for progressing material orders which will enable action to be taken before damage is done by late deliveries or delayed operations. In order to consider timing, sequencing and progress on contracts effectively, it is essential to produce a contract programme which relates to resource needs and in particular material requirements.

Mention should be made of the case study company which is typical of many small companies in its approach to work planning. It does produce pre-tender programmes in a very simplified form to aid the production of estimates and tenders. However these are not reviewed or re-drafted ready for use as management tools on live contracts. Buying operations are not coordinated through a central contract programme but are instigated by site on a day-to-day basis. There is clearly a need to implement some forward thinking into the company's processes.

The first step in introducing this notion of forward thinking is to re-draft the pre-tender programme into a working document and to add delivery dates to the approximate starting times and event sequencing which are already shown. It is not the object of this book to dwell on planning and programming matters, but it is important to realise that once a contract has been awarded it is vital to marshal the resources required. This can be effectively communicated through a well considered method statement and contract programme. From these two documents a buyer can draw up a schedule for all the materials and approximate starting dates for sub-contractors.

A key objective of this book is to consider how information can be related and integrated through a company's different management systems, and to this end it is useful first to reference information across documents (see Figure 4.3) and then to create a master control document which relates time, methods and resources, as shown in Figure 4.4. The procedure is as follows:

- Approximate dates for delivery should be given with the order. The duration of the delivery period should also be indicated.
- By keeping a careful eye on the programme and delivery schedule and by liaison with site the buyer can contact the supplier at a pre-determined time prior to the scheduled delivery date. This acts as a memory-jogging device to bring the impending delivery to the notice of the supplier. It is at this stage that a check is made to ensure that the supplier is still in a position to comply with the original or any new date set. The length of time allowed between contact with a supplier and a deadline for delivery will depend on the level of uncertainty about a supplier's ability to deliver on time. This is where an awareness of current market conditions becomes important. The frequency that reminders of impending delivery are sent out will depend on the experience of the supplier concerned.
- The copy order should also be filed under dates at which progress action will need to be taken. Requisitions from site should also be referenced against the timings detailed on the orders to ensure efficient communications occur.
- It is also useful to use an index card system (if the company is not computerised) which records the anticipated progressing action and the positive or negative result.

Inherent within the operation of the above system will be the provision of information, in particular, where a supplier is unable to comply with the company's requirements. Records from the system also provide indications as to the integrity and helpfulness of the particular supplier in attempting to, on the one hand, meet agreed target dates

Contract:
Project Nr:
Prepared by:

Nr:
Date:
Ref. Nr:

Dwg Nr/B of Q Ref. Programme Ref.	Material Description	Measured Quantity	Delivery Date(s)	Materials Received Sheet Ref.	Quantity Delivered	Quantity to be Delivered	Final Quantity	% Waste	Remarks

Figure 4.4 Material schedule and reconciliation statement

and, on the other, surmount contract difficulties.

It is imperative that the buyer keeps in close contact with the site in respect of purchasing progress and of any action taken or required to be taken. This is an important two-way communication system and it is suggested that a regular weekly review exercise is instigated between site and head office.

Receiving and checking

Receiving and checking materials is an important exercise which is generally not given enough attention by site personnel. A responsible person should be given the tasks of:

- Checking that a consignment of materials is in line with pre-determined guidelines. If the consignment does fall short of requirements then it is important to decide what is to be done as early as possible, especially if this could affect payment procedures.
- A materials received sheet should then be produced detailing the description, quantity and any problems of the materials delivered. For example, if only part of a consignment is acceptable then any action taken (partial acceptance) should be detailed, as this will have two ramifications:
  1. Progress action must be taken to remedy the supply problem.
  2. The accounts department should be warned to either expect a credit note or a reduced invoice taking account of the rejection of part of a delivery.

Liaison between site and head office is, as already mentioned, very important and head office will rely on information from site to ensure that action is taken as and when necessary. The weekly review process should include the updating and cross-referencing of materials schedules, ensuring that regular reconciliation exercises are pursued. It should not be forgotten that the accounts department should be kept abreast of information on a need-to-know basis so that payments to suppliers are maintained at the correct level, ensuring effective cashflow management for the company and supplier alike.

Summary

Emphasis has been placed upon systems and procedures and not the people who perform these functions.

Procurement (for the contracting organisation) should be seen as starting at the estimating and tendering stage, because the decisions taken at this stage become the benchmarks against which effective purchasing will be measured.

Companies should clearly identify their procurement objectives and keep these in mind throughout the systems operated.

In order to meet company purchasing objectives an intelligence system needs to be operated which allows information to be assimilated in respect of market's and supplier's operations. An understanding of current market trends is very important for effective purchasing. Three basic approaches to purchasing can be identified, however these should be seen as a means to an end, that of achieving objectives, and thus the approach should suit the contract circumstances.

The most useful approach to organising the purchasing function is to adopt a centralised/decentralised system. With such a stance, benefits can be gained as a result of the advantages of flexibility.

The three key elements to any purchase are quality, price/cost and delivery (time factor). Experience has shown that it is rare to satisfy all three elements against contract targets. If one were to prioritise then clearly quality must always be achieved; the other two elements must be measured against market trends and contract circumstances.

5 Plant Management

Introduction

It is difficult to identify the limit to machine usage on construction sites. It is clear, however, that as time goes by more machines will be invented or adapted for use in the construction of buildings. This being the case it is very important to attempt to measure the benefits or potential benefits of machine usage in particular circumstances. Managers are continually having to make decisions about methods of operation and the right mix of men and machines within a working environment. Machines are therefore selected, arrive on site, are used and, when a project is completed, removed and returned to the company's plant depot or the hire company. Within this cycle various decisions and assessments are required to be made. This chapter examines how to identify the need for machinery to suit particular circumstances, and how to measure its efficiency in use. A key aspect of plant management is the knowledge of where a machine is, what it is doing and how efficiently it is working, and this is an underlying theme of this chapter.

Categories of plant and equipment

There are three main categories under which equipment might be grouped, each bringing its own management problems:

- Small plant (non-mechanical or mechanical).
- Large plant (non-mechanical or mechanical).
- Administrative and sundry equipment.

It is worth listing some of the plant and equipment which might be classified under the above headings so that, as the management of equipment is examined, the particular problems associated with items in any of the groupings can be discussed.

Small plant

Non-mechanical

- Barrows, buckets, drums
- Spades, picks, trowels, hods
- Ropes, chains, pulleys, hoses
- Tampers, hammers, chisels, crowbars, cutters, screwdrivers
- Ladders, steps, trestles
- Tarpaulins, dust sheets

These examples have certain attributes which can cause problems for managers. They can be easily removed from site and in many cases this does not become apparent at an early enough stage to take the necessary action. All appear at first sight to be maintenance free, although this is clearly not the case. As a result they are used heavily or even misused, and therefore tend to have a very short working life or, more critically, become dangerous.

Mechanical

- Electric drills, sanders, grinders
- Power saws, routers

As with non-mechanical items these can easily be stolen. An important factor with small mechanical items is that they need regular maintenance and checking to ensure they are working safely. However, because of their size and the technology used in their manufacture this is normally a specialist operation, and often required to be carried out by the manufacturer or its agents. Frequently spare parts are unavailable, for a number of reasons, and if the machine is damaged through misuse it will not be repaired but will need to be replaced.

Large plant

Non-mechanical

- Scaffolding – tubular or proprietary
- Formwork – traditional or proprietary
- Shoring, hoarding, gantries
- Trench timbering, sheeting and jacks

Scaffolding is yet another item of plant which can easily be removed from site, and in this case it can be very difficult to identify even if it is eventually found. All the items listed are generally not looked after very well on site, and in consequence the cost of replacement to companies and the industry as a whole is very high. Sensible management procedures which ensure maximum security and use of these items will clearly benefit companies.

Mechanical

- Concrete mixers
- Transportation – lorries, dumpers, fork-lift trucks
- Cranes
- Excavators
- Dozers, graders
- Pumps
- Compressors
- Rollers
- Demolition equipment – breakers, crushers, pneumatic drills

The key issue here is maintenance. A regular programme of servicing is essential if the maximum safe use of these items of plant is to be achieved.

Administrative and sundry equipment

- Site hutting – offices, toilets, etc.
- Tables, chairs, cabinets
- Lighting and heating equipment
- Surveying equipment
- Compounds, fencing
- Helmets, gloves, goggles, boots, protective clothing

The majority of these items can normally be used effectively for long periods and transferred from site to site. However they all require to be stored when not in use. This is normally a problem if there is no job requiring their use and especially during periods of downturn in the industry.

Economics of plant usage

As costs rise, especially labour costs relative to the overall cost of construction, the need to find new construction methods becomes more and more important. In theory (provided conditions are right), by reducing the labour content and using machines to augment or replace labour, productivity should increase and result in cost reductions.

In simple terms the relationship to be achieved is:

$\downarrow$ LABOUR = $\uparrow$ PLANT = $\uparrow$ PRODUCTIVITY = COST $\downarrow$

It is often argued, and is certainly true when compared with many other industries, that the construction industry is not sufficiently 'capital intensive' to be effective in unfavourable economic conditions, such as recession. A capital-intensive industry is one that tends to invest money in machines rather than labour. However it must be said that this argument is normally put forward by economists who do not really appreciate the nature of construction activities. The nature of the industry was examined in chapter 2 and although it must be accepted that there is considerable scope for more mechanisation in both on-site and off-site production, it must also be appreciated that a construction site and the products produced on it are generally inherently different from factory production processes. In a factory, machines can be used for long uninterrupted periods (in car production, processes are spread over three 8-hour shifts with machines working 24 hours per day) so the relative machine cost falls against the overall cost of an operation. The same obviously applies to the use of machines in the construction industry, although the opportunities are more limited – if machines are to be cost-effective they must be operating gainfully for as many hours as possible. There is however a trade-off to be considered in terms of utilisation, operating costs, depreciation, productivity and obsolesence. Figures 5.1 and 5.2 show the relationships between these criteria and how they might be traded off in a given set of circumstances.

Having selected methods which are more machine orientated than labour intensive, the next problem for a manager is whether to buy or hire a machine. In chapter 2 the ability of the small builder to hire both large and small items of plant and equipment from the well-developed national network of plant hire organisations was identified. If such a supply network exists, why should any builder consider the purchase of plant and equipment, thus tying up capital and incurring the need to store and maintain these items?

Methods of obtaining plant and equipment

Plant and equipment may be obtained by one of the following methods:

(1) Hiring from a plant hire company – open to all companies irrespective of size.
(2) Hiring from the company's own plant department at a specified

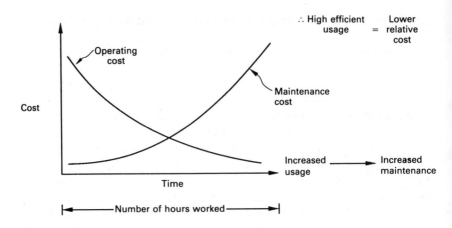

Figure 5.1   Relationship between operating costs and utilisation

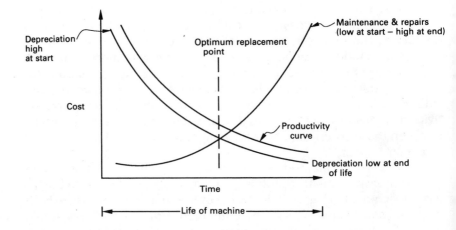

Figure 5.2   Relationship between obsolescence, depreciation and productivity

rate per hour/day/week. This assumes that the company, no matter how small, operates a plant section and has invested in the management of such a department. Many small to medium sized companies own equipment, although there is a difference between merely owning and using equipment, and investing in the efficient management of plant.

(3) Buying plant when required with the full cost being charged to a contract. This contract receives the credit at a later date if the machine is revalued after being returned to plant holding or is

sold. This approach locks money into an investment and requires a clear set of parameters for purchase, use and disposal to be established. Generally this approach should be reserved for larger long-term contracts carried out by larger, more sophisticated organisations.

Balance between owning and hiring

The decision here is dependent on particular conditions, but generally the following maxims apply:

'BUY' ⟶ Long and continued use

'HIRE' ⟶ Short-term basis

⟶ To get over peak production periods

Some of the issues to be taken into account are:

- Regardless of whether a machine is bought or hired, forecasts must be made about future work load and commitments.
- It is economic madness to own all the plant that will be needed.
- For a company developing a plant ownership policy it is good practice to buy machines which can be regularly used on most sites. Then, if needs dictate, acquire those machines of a specialist nature that give commercial advantage to the company.
- Machines which are owned need a maintenance provision.
- A plant holding of any size entails capital being locked up for long periods of time; this capital might be more profitably invested elsewhere.
- A plant holding requires premises for use as a plant yard and workshop.
- Controlling and maintaining machinery is a specialist function. Has the company the expertise or can it afford to acquire it?
- A company-owned machine tends to be retained beyond its efficient life, with consequent bad affects upon productivity and costs; clearly this should be guarded against.
- Normally transportation will be required to and from sites, and this may need to be of a specialist nature.

Plant selection and utilisation

The CIOB's Site Management Checklist No. 1 [15] puts forward a useful *aide-memoire* for a systematic approach to plant selection. Some of the ideas from this checklist are as follows:

(1) The task to be carried out should be analysed into its component parts (for particularly complex activities it is useful to adopt a work study approach):
(a) Type and method of operation.
(b) Materials to be used, together with any problems associated with their use.
(c) Working conditions, e.g. ground conditions or environment.
(d) Output required. This must be related to a contract programme.
(e) Working space available and limits on operation, e.g. noise.
(f) What ancillary operations are required, e.g. scaffolding/loading bays.

(2) Availability of plant:
(a) List available plant which is of suitable type and output.
(b) What is its availability, e.g. owned/hired/usage?
(c) What does it cost per hour?
(d) Classify its suitability for use under given conditions.
(e) List other items required as ancillary to the operation.

(3) Compare costs:
(a) Hire, buy or calculate costs of existing stock owned.
(b) Cost the whole operation, including ancillary items and, if hired, take account of any owned plant remaining unused.
(c) Convert costs to unit of measure, e.g. m^3, m^2.
(d) Compare costs with unit rates.

(4) Select plant.

(5) Servicing and maintenance:
(a) Ensure that only competent operatives service equipment.
(b) Ensure that plant records are kept – this will assist planned maintenance and should assist in planning 'return to yard' dates.
(c) Try to ensure that servicing and maintenance are carried out when the machine is not required for use.
(d) All plant, in order to ensure effective use, requires regular maintenance. Ensure that it gets it – any breakdown time should be recorded.

The points listed might at first sight just seem like common sense. However the busy site manager when faced with an urgent request for a machine may not appreciate the need or be inclined to go through a systematic process of selection.

To help site managers who may be under pressure, the checklist given could be turned into a simple pro-forma which initially aids selection. This could then be used in the management process to monitor usage, cost and cost benefit in terms of usefulness. Figure 5.3 illustrates how this might be achieved.

Having selected a machine to perform a specific task, it is clearly important to maintain records of how well the operation is progressing and how well the selected piece of equipment is performing. It is perhaps just as important to record when it is no longer required so that it can either be taken off-hire or moved to its next place of work. It should also be remembered that for machines to operate efficiently they require regular planned maintenance, and the best time for this to be done is when the item of plant is not required on site.

Plant records and costs

Whether a machine is owned or hired, the following aspects should be borne in mind by both owner and user:

(1) The frequency and cost of machine breakdowns on site should be minimised.
(2) Expenditure on maintenance, repairs and overhauls must be controlled.
(3) Capital locked up in plant ownership and back-up systems (e.g. spares) should be as low as possible, bearing in mind efficient and effective plant operation.
(4) Control and minimise the time required to be spent on repair and maintenance operations.

The only way to achieve the above objectives is through an efficient recording and analysis system which clearly identifies where a machine is, what it is doing, how efficiently it is working and at what cost.

Each item of equipment will require a reference card (computer database reference) on which its history from purchase to disposal should be recorded.

The basic records should cover the following:

(a) Type and make.
(b) Maker's serial number.
(c) Contractor's register number.
(d) Date of purchase.
(e) Supplier's name.
(f) Purchase price.
(g) Reference to specification and spares manual.
(h) Record of plant movements. It is a good idea to use a schedule format.
(i) Estimated life of the machine.

(1) *Work to be carried out*
    (i)   Method statement: ....
                                              ....
                                            ....

    (ii) Working conditions: ....
                                              ....
                                            ....

    (iii) Ancillary facilities   ....
            e.g. scaffolding: ....
                                              ....

    (iv) Output required (P) with ....
           reference to programme   ....
           and tender: ....

(2) *Plant selection*
    (i)   Identify and list: ....
           plant options   ....
           (include manufacturers/suppliers ....
           suggested outputs)   ....

    (ii) Cost comparisons: ....
           Cost/hour   ....
           Cost/unit (P)   ....
           Cost/operation   ....

    (iii) Cost ancillary facilities: ....
                                              ....
                                            ....
                                            ....
                                            ....

(3) *Utilisation log*: Summary from allocation sheets

Wk nr	Hours worked	Hours standing	Hours broken down	Actual output (A)	Variance A − P	Unit cost (A)	Variance A − P	Comments
1								
2								
3								
4								

A = Actual
P = Planned

Figure 5.3 Plant selection and utilisation pro-forma (for use of Site Manager and Surveyor)

(j) Estimated dates of overhauls. Again it is a good idea to present a schedule.
(k) Estimated utilisation – schedule showing any variances against actual utilisation.
(l) Actual utilisation.
(m) Budget upkeep costs.
(n) Actual upkeep costs. Analysis of any variances required here.
(o) Estimated date of sale or point at which machine is obsolete.
(p) Assumed sale price or scrap value.

It is from these records that information in respect of cost benefit in terms of value for money and return to the company can be assessed, and as such they should form part of an integrated resource and cost management system. Chapter 9 follows up this approach and discusses how plant costs are identified and managed within a budget.

Summary

Any contracting organisation needs either the services of a diverse plant hire sector of the industry or its own efficient plant department.

Sites are looking for readily available equipment which is fully maintained and will not let them down.

It is the site's responsibility to ensure that, through adequate forward planning, machines are economically used.

The longer the working (efficient) life of a machine, the cheaper the operating cost becomes.

By careful and proper use and avoidance of misuse, the machine is kept in good condition and consequently its useful working life is prolonged.

The only way a company can evaluate the cost benefit of plant usage is via an efficient record and analysis system.

6 Sub-contract Management

Introduction

In chapter 1 the reasons why significant amounts of the work on projects are sublet were discussed. On some contracts all the work might be sub-contracted. It is difficult to envisage a time when companies will return to employing high levels of labour, especially when there are many companies providing a full range of construction services in the market place, and bearing in mind that both risk and cost can be minimised if careful sub-contract arrangements are made.

Sub-contractors have become a major control aspect on the majority of contracts and can make up a large proportion of the cost element of what is termed 'builder's own work'.

Generally speaking there are two distinct categories of sub-contract organisation offering services in construction markets, namely labour-only subcontractors and labour-and-material sub-contractors. Sometimes both types are referred to as domestic sub-contractors to distinguish them from nominated sub-contractors. However, irrespective of how one might classify these service organisations, the administrative and management considerations are similar.

The key factor to establish is the service being offered and the limits of such service. From this the extent of facilities and assistance required to be provided by the contractor can be established. The sub-contract agreement should set out the agreed level of provision by both parties. This chapter is concerned with the satisfactory administration and management of the sub-contract process.

It is sound practice to monitor the intermediate financial position of any project and to establish financial trends to allow corrective or possible contractual action to be taken. It is with this in mind that a structured approach to the procurement of sub-contracts and the management of sub-contractors' accounts are put forward in this chapter.

The twin themes of cost and cashflow management will be introduced and examined as tools in the overall sub-contract management process.

Selection

It can be argued that the selection of suitable sub-contract organisations should start prior to even considering projects to be carried out. The ideal would be for a database of suitable companies to be established, in order that selection of the 'right' sub-contractor to suit particular circumstances on contracts can be managed effectively.

Our case study company will be seeking to make decisions about the use of sub-contractors in two situations, namely when it tenders for work in competition and for its own speculative projects. In the first case, decisions about the level of work to be sublet will be made at the tender stage and quotations from sub-contractors will set the budget levels for sections of the contract. In the second instance, the company will need to establish a budget for the speculative project and then it will seek to obtain quotations from sub-contractors which fall within its budget aspirations. In both cases, suitable companies will be required to provide quotations which can be relied upon and which can form the basis of a contractual agreement on a live project.

The administrative and management process therefore starts at the pre-tender or pre-contract stage as an estimate or budget is being developed.

The first step in the selection process should be the setting up and maintenance of a register of sub-contractors.

Register of sub-contractors

Such a register will enable effective checking procedures to be carried out in the following areas.

- Financial stability – this can only be indicative, and will of necessity be based on a company's published accounts which are generally out of date. Nevertheless trends can be identified and questions asked.
- Work capabilities – past contracts can be reviewed and references taken up.
- Level of operations – an approximation of how much work a company can handle efficiently at any time should be assessed.

The following aspects should be included and regularly updated on each sub-contractor's record card:

(1) Area of operations and ability to move around.
(2) Size and type of work capable of being done.
(3) Labour and supervisory resources available.
(4) Record of work previously carried out.
(5) References from: (a) trade source, (b) professional source, (c) bank/financial source.
(6) Insurance cover.

It is important that registers of this nature are regularly updated and notes/remarks added to show:

(a) Performance – an honest appraisal.
(b) Site feedback information – production and financial.
(c) Records and details of contracts successfully carried out together with existing workload of the company.
(d) Adverse comments where applicable – again an honest 'objective' view.
(e) Names of senior and supervisory staff for contact and action purposes.

It is also good practice to add/subtract names in line with current market opportunities and feedback and analysis of performance.

It is from this register that prospective sub-contractors are chosen to receive enquiries for quotations.

It is important to send out a number of enquiries for the following reasons:

• To gain competitive prices on economic grounds.
• To maintain tendering integrity.
• To avoid complacency and to ensure realistic bids.

The number of enquiries sent out will depend on market conditions, however experience show that four achieve the above objectives and are also manageable.

Enquiry stage

The Code of Estimating Practice [16] puts forward the information which should be given to sub-contractors at the enquiry stage in order that they can produce effective quotations:

(1) Copies of the relevant drawings, specifications and bill of quantity pages covering or allied to the work to be quoted for.
(2) Whether the quotation is to be for labour and material or on a labour-only basis.

(3) Plant and equipment to be provided by the main contractor and what the sub-contractor will have to supply for itself.
(4) Anticipated commencement and completion dates for the sub-contract work, work programme and sequences.
(5) Brief description of the project and how the sub-contract work fits in with the overall programme of events.
(6) Site address.
(7) Name of client.
(8) Names and addresses of the architect, quantity surveyor and other consultants, where applicable.
(9) Form of sub-contract to be used.
(10) Important aspects of the main contract which the sub-contractor should be aware of.
(11) Any general conditions, specifications or drawings which the sub-contractor will be required to adhere to.
(12) Place where and time when documentation can be inspected.
(13) Whether a firm or variable price is required.
(14) Terms of payment.
(15) The main contractor's terms and conditions which would form part of any agreements reached.
(16) Period for which quotation should remain open for acceptance.
(17) Date for submission.
(18) Contact in main contractor's organisation.

Receipt and adjudication of quotations

The key aspects to consider at this stage are:

- A systematic review and comparison of quotations received to enable one set of prices to be selected for inclusion in an estimate (at the tender stage) or to enable negotiations to proceed at the contract stage. The Code of Estimating Practice [16] provides some useful pro-formas for comparison purposes.
- The selection of a sub-contractor for further negotiations and subsequent contractual agreement. This need not be the sub-contractor whose quotation was used at the tender stage. The decision will depend on a number of factors, not least on market considerations in terms of price level and availability.

The systematic check should cover the following:

- That all items have been considered and priced.
- That all items are priced correctly and in accordance with the unit of measurement and that they closely relate to other similar items within the quotation.

- That the rates are realistic and are comparable with those of competitors.
- That all conditions have been complied with.
- That no variations or qualifications have been made which do not comply with the specification or details sent to the sub-contractor.
- That the sub-contractor has accepted the terms and conditions of the proposed contract and has not substituted his own conditions or qualified his quotation. (An example of where conditions might be in conflict is when sub-contractors or suppliers refer to their own conditions for use. These 'feint grey print conditions' are often printed on the back of quotations. Great care must be exercised here.)
- That all additions, extensions and collations are correct.

Any errors or discrepancies should be referred back to the sub-contractor for clarification and correction.

Automatic choice of the lowest quotation is not recommended. An estimator, in the first instance, must have the ability to judge, within reasonable limits, a 'right' and 'wrong' price. Above all, he must have the judgement and knowledge to interpret preambles, bill descriptions and measurement to determine what should be included in a price.

Before rates from a quotation can be included in an estimate, the following should be considered and allowances made to cover expected costs arising from some or all of the following items:

(1) Unloading of materials and by whom.
(2) Protection and security of materials.
(3) Provision of storage facilities.
(4) Provision of plant and use of scaffolding and other preliminary items.
(5) Use of power.
(6) Protection of the finished work and responsibility.
(7) Main contractor's supervision and liaison with sub-contractor's management.
(8) Overheads and profit, where applicable.
(9) Risk and contingencies, if considered necessary.

The estimator should now be in a position to include rates in the estimate for the sub-contract work.

The next point at which decisions in respect of sub-contractors are required is on the award of a contract.

Many changes could have occurred between the time when a tender was submitted and the point at which it is accepted, or even the point at which sub-contract services are required. For example, the markets might have changed so drastically that the original sub-contractor is now not prepared to enter into an agreement. It is therefore important to ensure at the contract stage that all the sub-contractors participating at the tender stage are still prepared to enter into agreements based on their original quotations, or whether re-quotations will be required. Whichever is the case, the next step is to gain contractual agreement and to sanction the selection process ready for employment on site.

Post-contract selection

It is always a good idea to review the selection process at the tender stage and to gain general agreement as to the use of a particular sub-contractor. Figure 6.1 is an example of a sub-contract approval pro-forma for use in this process.

This pro-forma allows the review of pre-tender and post-contract decision-making. It identifies the quotations received at the tender stage and the one selected for use within the tender. Re-quotations can also be compared with the quotation levels exhibited at the tender stage which allows the potential buying margins to be assessed.

Another important aspect of the pro-forma is the approvals and documentation checking mechanism whereby key individuals or departments of the company check and approve various aspects of the selection process. This has the dual effects of validating and gaining acceptance of the final choice.

Having selected and gained contractual agreement with a sub-contractor, the on-site control process commences.

The principal control mechanism will be that of managing and exerting financial control over the sub-contractor. That is, ensuring that payments are made against measured and acceptable works completed.

Principles of financial control

There are three main elements or objectives of financial control of sub-contractors:

- Cashflow management.
- Performance measurement.
- Feedback.

Cashflow

The payment of sub-contractors represents an outflow of money from the company to the sub-contractor and thus must be controlled

SUB-CONTRACT APPROVAL SHEET

MAIN CONTRACT ------------------------------   Nr --------------------------------
SUB-CONTRACT WORKS ---   (L/O – L&M)
Section A – To be completed by buyer/buying department

Quotations received:

	Name	Value	% on ICs	Remarks

Recommended
    2
    3
    4
    5
    6
Tender quotation
B of Q value

Papers to Surveyor/Managing Surveyor---------------- (date)

Section B – To be completed by Surveyor/Managing Surveyor

                                                               Remarks
1. Quotations checked for comparability ---
2. Recommended quotation check for:
    (a) Pricing consistency --
    (b) Conditions ---
    (c) Qualifications --
3. Any particular conditions to be incorporated into Sub-contract:
4. Ancipated Buying Margin (Gross)   £
    Deduct allowance for attendances
      and contingencies   £ ------------------
          Net Buying Margin   £ ------------------
Signed ---
              Papers   to   Contracts
Director -- (date)

Section C – To be completed by Contract Director

    Sub-contract period ---------------- weeks Anticipated start date ------------
    Sub-contractor's resources and records checked -------------------------------
    Position with S/C programme --
    Any other comments --
    Recommendation approved ---
    Papers returned to buyer --- (date)

Section D – Sub-contract documents

Completed (Buying Dept.) -- (date)
Final scrutiny -- Company Secretary
Documents despatched --- (date)
Signed by S/C -- (date)

Figure 6.1 Sample of sub-contract approval sheet

efficiently. The sub-contractor will need to receive money at a steady rate to meet commitments, and the main contractor will be concerned both with the well-being of the sub-contractor as well as his own.

Performance measurement

This has two aspects;

(a) Production performance.
(b) Financial performance.

Both of these are interrelated in that if a sub-contractor's production falls (as measured against planned performance) not only do his own financial returns fall but also those of the main contractors.

How then can each aspect be measured?

Production performance

Planned performance should be shown on the contract programme. The sub-contractor's planned performance should have been agreed at the negotiation stage and this should have been referenced to the main contract programme.

Actual performance on site should be recorded, agreed and referenced to the contract programme at regular and agreed intervals.

Together with regular meetings and communications with the sub-contractor, a trend of performance can be evaluated and regulated.

Financial performance

What is required here is a costed/valued programme. In other words the tender sum is broken down into its constituent parts and the costs/values are spread across the programme to produce a contract budget (see chapter 8 for examples of how this is accomplished).

Actual sub-contract costs/values are monitored at each payment cycle by measuring the work carried out and applying the agreed rates to the measured items. The outcome of this process is then compared with the budget to review achievement or non-achievement of target performance. It is also important to ensure that payments are made at the right level because both under- and over-payment can have serious consequences.

Feedback

Records covering individual items and type of work provide basic information which can be used in establishing future tendering requirements and data, and so enable future performance targets to be set.

However, technology in terms of both methods of operation and materials is constantly changing, and thus there is a continuing need to confirm and review hypothetical situations such as individual rates and sub-contractor tender levels.

Methods of financial control

Cashflow management

Sub-contract agreements set out the payment requirements which are normally interim payments during the progress of the work, enabling capital employed to be identified and controlled. The first step in cashflow management is to produce a payment profile for the sub-contract to be managed. This identifies the anticipated level and timing of payments against which actual payments can be monitored.

Payment control

Wherever possible sub-contractor payments should be linked and coincide with the main contractor's valuations. Thus when the main contractor is paid the sub-contractor should also be paid from receipts, a process which helps to produce strong 'cash-in' positions. Payments must be verified and should be backed up by measurement and valuation of the work actually carried out.

Depending on the nature of the contract, the method of verification may vary from a simple statement of the percentage of work completed to a fully re-measured and itemised interim account.

It is essential, whichever approach is adopted, that it should be submitted in written form so that it acts as a record and the submission is unambiguous.

Payments should always be backed up by measurements and calculations, 'payments on account' being avoided.

If upon checking a sub-contractor's valuation and application there is a disagreement, it is good practice to substantiate and produce calculations to illustrate any stance taken.

It is very important to keep up-to-date account details backed up by measurements and calculations in respect of:

(a) Measurement/re-measurement.
(b) Re-measurement of provisional items.
(c) Measurement of variations.
(d) Dayworks.
(e) Increased costs, where these apply.
(f) Claims – classified as agreed/not agreed.

Finally it is very important to manage retention funds effectively. It is normal for all payments to be subject to the deduction of a retention sum up to an agreed maximum limit.

At the time of practical completion and at the end of the defects liability period, retention releases are applicable. It is therefore important to ensure the correct level of release, so that the sub-contractor's account is up-to-date in respect of:

- Measured work.
- Agreed claims.
- Dayworks.
- Increased costs.
- Contra-charges.

It is very important at these stages to avoid the risk of over-payment and to ensure that an adequate retention fund is maintained to cover any works still required to be carried out by the sub-contractor.

CERTIFICATION OF PAYMENT TO SUB-CONTRACTOR

Contract:
Sub-contractor:
Payment Nr:
Details of payment: £   £
   Measured work
   Materials on site
   Dayworks
   Increased costs   _____   _____
                            £   £

Less retention %

                                                 _____

Less discount %

                                                 _____

Less contra-charges

                                                 _____

Less previous net payments

                                                 _____

                      Amount due   £

Authorised by _____   Date _____

Figure 6.2 Payment certificate

Figures 6.2 and 6.3 are examples of the use of payment certificates and payment record statements as a means of ensuring payments are processed effectively.

Summary

Sub-contractors play a major part in fulfilling contracts and therefore require specific management attention.

Because sub-contractors only owe contractual allegiance to the main contractor they may not understand or even care about the main contractor's broader objectives on a project, unless these are clearly identified.

It is vitally important to seek to control the selection process from the pre-tender or pre-contract stage of a project. It is at this stage that time, method and budget criteria are established, and it will be against such criteria that eventual profit or loss on projects will be measured.

The key elements of control are production performance, as measured against an agreed programme, and financial performance as measured against an agreed budget which not only identifies costs and values but also establishes a planned payment profile against which actual payments are monitored.

PAYMENT RECORD SHEET

Name:

Contract _____ Nr _____

Sub-contract:

Sub-contract value:

Terms of payment:

Application   *Authorisation*

App. Nr	Msd work	Dayworks MOS	I/C	Total	Running total	Cert Nr	Work exc.	Daywork MOS	I/C	T A

Figure 6.3 Payment record statement

7　Cost Classification

Introduction

Each of the resources discussed in earlier chapters carry cost implications which need to be considered in a variety of ways.

It is impossible to manage the costs that a company incurs as a single entity. They need to be classified in such a way that management can review the cost of an activity and groups of activities in order that decisions can be made in the light of variances from planned performance and budgeted cost.

The need to classify cost in a hierarchical fashion, so that cost elements become more meaningful and manageable, forms a central element of this chapter. Cost relationships at different operating levels should be identified, as a means of aiding integration within the management information systems required to be operated by a company.

Cost classification as an aid to control

A consistent approach to cost classification is vitally important. Costs can be grouped under selected headings and also classified at different levels within a company's cost administration system.

The important criterion for a company is that on selecting convenient classification headings and the levels at which measurement will take place, these selections are adhered to in order that sensible control is achieved and a database of information is maintained.

Costs can be classified as either:

(1) Past costs – those incurred by a company in the past and suitably classified under an appropriate heading, e.g. labour cost associated with hanging a door under given conditions. Such data are an essential ingredient of a feedback system and should be held until superseded by costs generated from more recently completed work.

(2) Current costs – these are costs being incurred on contracts, and as such are costs which are to be controlled within budget targets. The actual cost of carrying out the work is collected and compared with the estimator's forecast of cost made at the tender stage.

(3) Future costs – these are generated from past and current trading activity. For the company as a whole, next year's administrative and production costs can be forecast by the managing director, with the help of the company secretary, for use within a budgeting system. If a company's future cashflows are to be estimated then a method of future costing is essential. At the contract level, these are the estimated costs produced by the estimator.

If the above classifications are adopted then costs can be collected and subsequently extracted from the database as and when required. This is a central requirement of any cost control system.

Hierarchical approach to cost classification

Figure 7.1 illustrates the way in which costs can be classified and downgraded from the conglomerate costs incurred by the organisation as a whole, to the individual cost elements of resources used on site.

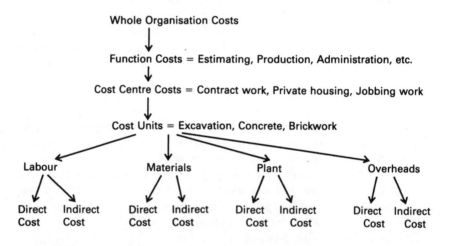

Figure 7.1 Cost classification downgrading system

A 'direct' cost, as shown in Figure 7.1, is any cost (the cost of a brick in a wall for instance) which can be assigned to a cost unit or cost centre. An 'indirect' cost cannot be directly assigned and will require apportioning across a range of cost units, e.g. transportation costs.

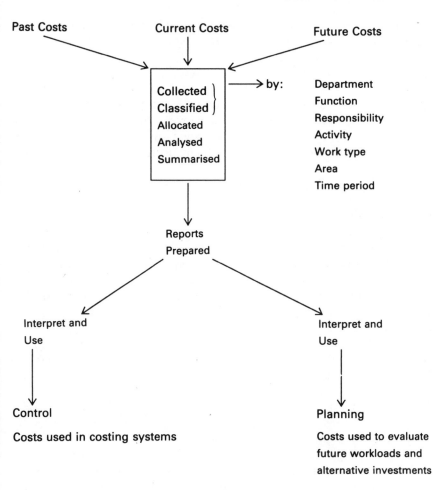

Figure 7.2   Requirements of a cost administration system

Requirements of a cost administration system

Figure 7.2 identifies the basic requirements of a cost administration system which allows cost data to be interpreted at the various levels identified in Figure 7.1, and which can then be used for planning and control purposes. The system illustrated in Figure 7.2 together with the hierarchical approach discussed above should enable a database to be managed on either a hierarchical or relational basis. Although this terminology is usually applied to database design for computers, it is, or has been, the basis of most good manual systems for many years [17].

If an efficient manual system can be established, subsequent computerisation will be done with greater ease.

Cost responsibility levels

Franks [18] advocates a corporate approach to control and illustrates this by means of responsibilities at each level. This then lends itself to a presentation of budget information down through the organisation and a reporting system back up eventually, in summary form, to board level.

Figure 7.3 is an illustration of this idea. Research has shown that it is difficult to differentiate between various levels of operation and responsibilities within a small building company (the case study company). The managing director may well take on several roles and perform a number of different functions. However, this does not mitigate against the use of an approach which differentiates between levels of responsibility in an organisation. In fact, for an effective control system to operate, costs must be classified under convenient headings and then somebody must be allocated responsibility for cost monitoring and control.

As identified above, it may be difficult to define clear responsibility levels in a smaller organisation. Nevertheless, such responsibility levels can be established. These provide a screening facility whereby cost information is collected and reports are produced which can then be compared with the relevant budgets.

Financial control procedures and systems

The estimate should be seen as the starting point for a company's cost-control considerations. If all of the tender sums for contracts won are added together this will represent the company's turnover for a given trading period. It must be stressed that a tender sum, a contract sum and amounts agreed at the final account stage will generally be different for many reasons. It is important to identify the difference between anticipated turnover and actual turnover. It should be remembered that some contracts straddle trading periods and this must be taken into account when accounts are prepared. The costs calculated within the estimate represent 'cost targets' against which 'actual costs' must be measured, the outcome of such comparisons represents profit or loss (planned/actual) on individual contracts and goes to make up company profit/loss. 'Cost' when converted into 'expenditure', by identifying when monies are expected to flow out of the organisation, represents the outflow aspect of the cashflow equation

Level	Cost Responsibilities	Cost Information	Information Flow
Board	Company turnover Profitability Overhead control Investments	A company budget is produced against which actual activity costs can be compared	
General Management	Overhead costs Pay accounts Secure work Set cost objectives Manage contracts Managers	Use of departmental and contract budgets as a comparative medium when receiving cost reports from contracts managers	
Contracts Management	Contract costs Set performance objectives	Comparison of cost allowed for in tender with actual cost on site on a regular basis	
Site Management	Contract costs	Actual cost as measured by allocation sheets and materials received sheets	

In the Information Flow column: Budget Information (downward arrow), Actual Cost Information (upward arrow), Cost Reporting.

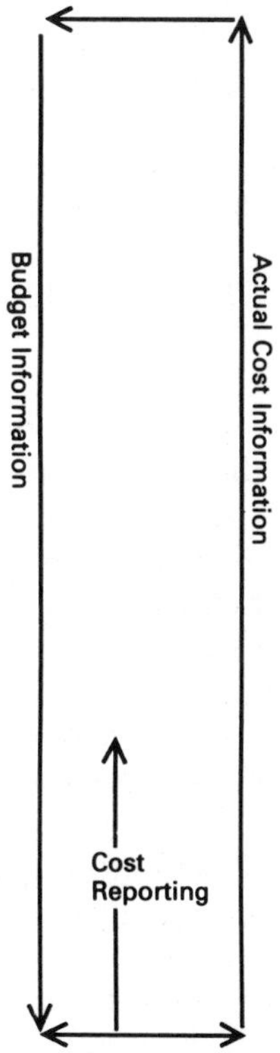

Figure 7.3   Cost responsibility levels

and as such must also be measured and monitored as a central component of a control system, especially if liquidity is to be managed effectively.

Some of the problems associated with financial control in the construction industry which perhaps do not exist in other manufacturing industries are:

(1) Design responsibility and therefore specification control are normally outside the control of the builder.
(2) A new production process is required to be set up for every job.
(3) Methods of operation will vary to suit individual circumstances.
(4) The offer to carry out work is based on written/drawn descriptions of the work, before production commences.

(5) The estimator establishes an 'estimated method' in a very short time scale (*The code of procedure for single stage selective tendering* (1986) suggests between four to six weeks should be allowed to tender for work), and this method is used to compare 'actual costs' for methods which might vary widely from those considered appropriate during estimating.
(6) The production process is made up of one-off, non-cyclic and short-duration tasks.
(7) The product or service can be varied during the production process to suit client requirements or unforeseen circumstances.

Even given these problems, the basic principles of cost control and the benefits derived from the use of such a system apply to all commercial organisations.

An example of the basic requirements of a control system is given below and can be used to evaluate the work required at each of the stages in its operation in subsequent chapters.

Cycle of events	Typical contract
(1) Formulation of plan	(1) Estimating and making an offer
(2) Monitoring actual progress against plan	(2) Using estimated costs and comparing these with actual costs
(3) Ascertaining causes of divergence from plan	(3) Setting out reasons against over/under-spending
(4) Taking corrective action	(4) Trying to reduce costs back within estimate
(5) Restatement or change of plan	(5) Stating the 'over-spending' in controllable terms and using this information to produce more efficient estimates in the future

Before going on to consider the attributes of a control system in detail, it is important to distinguish between the various levels at which financial reporting and cost control take place within a company.

(1) Company financial control system

All registered companies are required to keep 'proper books of account' [19], the summaries of which (Balance Sheet, Profit Statement, Sources and Application of Funds Statement) are prepared by the company accountant. The emphasis here is on conveying information to shareholders about the well-being of the company. These final statements, once audited and published via the Registrar of Companies, can be obtained by other companies or lending institutions that are associated or wish to trade (clients, banks, sub-contractors, suppliers, etc.) with the company.

They can be used to monitor financial performance, e.g. debt/credit levels, liquidity/solvency, etc. At present these accounts are historical documents and thus perform the role of an information system. Generally financial accounts are presented for the company as a whole.

(2) Overall company cost control system

In a large company this system might be designed and operated by a cost or management accounting department. In a small organisation this is usually the responsibility of the company secretary, who may be assisted by the accountant who prepares the financial statements previously mentioned. The emphasis is the supply of information to management to aid the monitoring and control of financial performance for the various functional areas within a company, e.g. production, estimating, buying, etc. Information produced can be used by the managing director and the board to aid the taking of decisions for future trading periods. Management accounts are presented in cost centre/cost unit format.

(3) Contract cost control system

The emphasis here is on the provision of timely information to site management in respect of contract progress and activity productivity in cost terms.

From this two important complementary functions can be performed:

(1) Forward planning of contracts with cost implications clearly stated.
(2) Feedback of information from site to the main control systems for future planning and estimating purposes.

These exercises would normally be the responsibility of a surveyor, or in a very small company, a contract supervisor/manager would be required to report on-site cost and value.

The three areas identified represent two internal and essentially forward-looking systems, which eventually provide information to draw up the accounts for the past year's trading of the company as a whole, together with one external reporting system.

Although the level of accuracy within each of the systems will vary, the same basic information is used. For example:

(1) Contract cost control – based on a forecast of cost at the tender stage against which weekly/monthly activity costs, of varying degrees of accuracy, are compared. The level of accuracy will depend on the methods used to collect the actual costs on site.

(2) Company cost control – based on reports from contracts, the level of accuracy increasing throughout the life of a contract. The nearer the final account date, the more accurate the cost information is likely to be.

(3) Financial control – based on the 'cost' and 'value' information extracted from a company's books. Thus when the final statements are produced a high level of accuracy should be achieved. However, it is the nature of the 'payment systems' operated in the construction industry which dictates this level of accuracy in a company's end of year figures [20]. The concept of 'long-term' contracts and 'payments on account', and how these are to be dealt with, can lead to a need for considered interpretation of future costs and values on contracts by the accountant [21], which may affect the accuracy of the final figures. Figure 7.4 illustrates the relationships which exist between cost and financial data collected and used within a company's financial control systems.

Summary

The central theme of this chapter has been that in order to control costs it is necessary to classify them under appropriate headings, and then consistently to describe and measure the cost of activities in the same way throughout the life of a contract and a trading period.

As a global approach it is useful to classify under the headings of past, current and future cost. The idea of using a hierarchical structure was put forward which allows activities and costs to be grouped in handlable packages. It also introduces the notion of levels, and from this the ability to filter information on a need-to-know basis can be developed. From these ideas the concept of responsibility and its relationship with control at a series of organisational levels is discussed.

The problems associated with operating financial control systems in the construction industry are presented and it is argued that, even though it may be more difficult to operate a structured approach on projects, it should nevertheless not detract from the benefits to be derived in attempting to provide structure.

The basic ingredients of the system are then presented and the three key company systems, namely company financial control, overall company cost control and contract cost control, are identified. These are discussed in more detail in the following chapters.

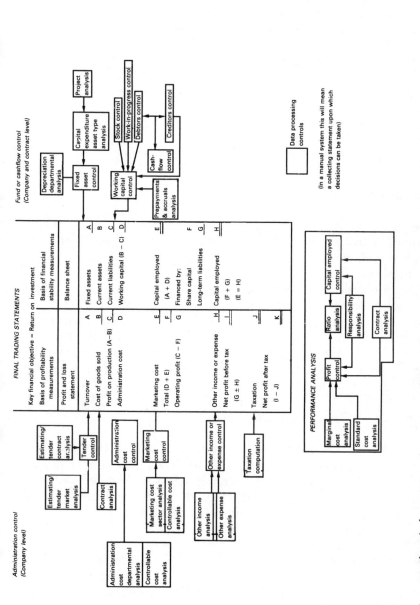

Figure 7.4 Accounting information for control [after Thornton N., *Management Accounting*, Heinemann, 1978]

8   Cost Monitoring

Introduction

The need consistently to classify, record, measure and compare planned activities and costs with actual events and actual costs has been identified as vitally important if management is to make sensible financial decisions in the light of current trading trends.

The problems of consistent recording and measurement will be examined and approaches to improving the validity of cost data collection will be suggested. In chapter 7 the estimate was put forward as the starting point for a company's cost-control considerations. This idea is taken further in this chapter where the links between estimating and cost control are examined with a view to designing an integrated financial control system.

Estimating and its links with cost control

In chapter 1 it was established that once an offer has been made and accepted by a client, the tender sum becomes the contract sum and this is the reference against which profit or loss is measured. It was also established that the way a company produces its estimates has a great deal to do with the information provided by the tender documentation or the way information is handled by the estimator.

Also, there will be a need to refer to performance data which is derived essentially from historical sources or synthesised from first principles, again using data probably collected historically. This being the case, such feedback information from whatever source needs to be critically reviewed.

Three basic approaches to producing estimates (see chapter 1) can be identified. The approach adopted will be dependent on the level of information provided and the level of expertise exhibited by the person producing the estimate. The approaches are:

Analytical estimating
Operational estimating
Time and materials estimating

Foster [22] presents a picture of how estimating skills are acquired by trial and error or by experiential learning.

Another factor to bear in mind is the amount of time devoted to producing estimates. This must have a bearing on the amount of detail in the final product.

However the estimate is produced, in order to operate cost monitoring exercises, data must be capable of being interpreted or transformed into cost information that is readily comparable.

The following are examples of the ways in which estimators might build up their rates. Common work descriptions are used to present each of the estimating approaches:

A. Half brick wall in skin of hollow wall built fair and pointed
   one side in cement lime mortar (1:1:6)   118 m²
B. Half brick wall in skin of hollow wall in multi-colour
   facing bricks (£180 per thousand delivered to site) in
   stretcher bond built fair and flush pointing as the work
   proceeds in cement lime mortar (1:1:6)   125 m²
C. Form 50 mm cavity of hollow walls, inc. three wall ties
   per square metre   120 m²
D. Close 50 mm cavity of hollow walls with brickwork half
   brick thick   20 m

Figure 8.1 illustrates how the above items might be priced using an analytical approach. Note that each activity is considered separately with the individual resources analysed in detail. Implied within the analysis is a method of carrying out the work.

Figure 8.2 demonstrates an operational approach to pricing the same four items. In this case the four separate activities are considered as one operation, that of building a cavity wall.

Figure 8.3 takes a time and materials stance. It must be appreciated that there are no set guidelines for this method, although Foster [22] does explain how he acquired a working knowledge of this type of approach.

Each of the approaches produces an estimate of net cost which can either be a lump sum across the four activities or presented as a rate against each activity. The analytical approach attempts to identify each element of a resource cost in detail and relies on individual output constants to bring method and cost together. The operational approach groups the four activities and then attempts to apply an

A)

Labour £	Material £	Plant £	Net Unit rate £
1 Brick'l'er at £5·00 = 5·00 ½ lab. at £4·50 = 2·25 Gang rate 7·25	Flettons at £109/1000 on site ∴ 59 No. in m² ½B 3 + waste 5% 62 at 10p/brick = 6·20	S/3½(0·1⅟0·1·0) mixer. Hire/wk. = 20·00 lab. in ch. 4·50 + 1p w.s.a. × 40 = 180·40 200·40	Lab 11·33 Mat. + plant 7·64 18·97
No. of bks/m² × G.r ───────────── output 59 ── × £7·25 = 8·55 50 Pointing as work proceeds = 3m²/hr. ∴ 1 m² every 20 mins ∴ ⅓ × 7·25 = 2·41 10·96	Mortar (as calc) Machine mix (1:1:6) 1 m³ cement on site = 92·88 1 m³ lime on site = 46·47 6 m³ sand at £20 = 120·00 Add – Shrinkage 25% 259·35 Waste 5% 77·80 337·15 ∴ by parts in mix (8) £42·14/m³ Add mach cost 6·24 Mat + plant £48·38	Machine used 37 hrs ∴ 3 hrs. standing time ∴ cost/hr = 200·40 ÷ 37 = 5·41 ½ hr/day C+M = ⅟16 × 4·51 = 28	
Fair face lab selecting bricks 5 mins at £4·50 37 £11·33	Material in m² = 0·029m³ ∴ 0·029 at 48·38 = 1·40 + waste 0·04 1·44 Add bricks 6·20 7·64	1·14 litres petrol at 40p = 45 oil and grease = 10 6·24 1 m³/hr for lime mix ∴ Cost of mixer per m³ = 6·24	

B)

Labour	Material		Net Unit rate
59 ── × 7·25 = 12·22 35 Pointing as work proceeds = 1·70m²/hr ∴ 7·25 ──── = 4·26 1·70 Fair face 5 mins at £4·50 = 0·37 Lab/m² 16·85	Facings 180·00 Unload 15·00 on site 195·00 ∴ 62 No. at 0·195 12·09 Motor a.b. 1·44 Material/plant/m² 14·53		Lab 16·85 M+P 14·53 £ 31·38

C)

Labour	Material		Net Unit rate
C) 1 bricklayer setting and clearing 12m² of cavity/hr ∴ ⅟12 × £5·00 41p/m²	Wall ties ~ 10 p ea. ∴ 3 × 10 = 30 + 10% waste = 3 33		Lab 41p Mat 33 74p/m²

D)

Labour	Material		Net Unit rate
D) Gang rate = 7·25 ∴ 5 m/hr ∴ ⅕ × 7·25 = 1·45/m	Allow 5 bricks per metre incl. waste ∴ 5 at 0·10 = 50 Mortar, say 10 60p/m		Lab 1·45 Mat 60 £2·05/m

Figure 8.1   Example of analytical estimating

Basic Data

A - Skin in commons - 118m² = 6962 bricks
B - Skin in facings - 125m² = 7375 bricks
                                14337 bricks

If one man lays 4725 bricks/8 hr. day, then
brickwork will take 30½ days (allowing for stoppages)
              ∴ 2men = 16 days

C - Form cavity - 120m² as work proceeds
D - Close cavity - 20m² as work proceeds

Labour Allowance

Method: 2+1 gang with manual unloading.
Normal 8 hr. day with no overtime

Time assessment for operations/day	Lab.hrs.	Crafr hours
1. Labour unloading mats.	1·00	
2. Loading out for B/h	3·50	
3. Operating mixer	2·00	
4. B/L sorting out work (inc. cavity)		1·00
5. Rake out and point as work proceeds		1·50
6. Selecting bricks for fair face	0·50	
7. Allowance for stoppages - lunch, tea	1·00	1·00
8. Laying bricks		4·50
	8·00	8·00

∴ 2 x 8 hrs x £5.00 = £ 80
  1 x 8 hrs x £4·50 = £ 37
                        £ 117 Gang cost per day
              Total labour cost of operations
              - 16 x £117   = £1872·00

Materials

Commons = 6962
+ 5% waste = 348   7310 at 10p = 731·00
  Facings   7375
+ 5% waste   369   7744 at 18p = 1393·92

Mortar = 0.029 x 243 m² x £42·14/m³ = 296·96
        + waste and clsg. 3%   = 8·91
Wall ties 3 x 243 m² x 10p x (+10% waste) = 80·20
100 bks. (car'clsg) at 10p   = 10·00
              Total material cost = £2520·99
                          cfd. £4392·99 [continued]

Figure 8.2 Example of operational estimating

bfd. £4392·99

Plant Allowance

5/3½ (0·14/0·10l) mixer at £20 per wk = 20·00
lab. in charge £4·50 + 1p wra. at 40hrs.=180·40
                                          200·00

Machine used 37hrs. ∴ 3hrs. standing time
∴ Cost/hr. = 200·40 ÷ 37   = 5·41
½hr/day Clean + Maint. ⅟₁₆ x 4·51 = ·28
1·14 litres petrol at 40p   = ·45
        Oil and grease   = ·10
Output = 1m³/hr.   Cost/m³   = 6·24

∴ 7m³ x £6·24 = Machine cost   =   43·68
                    Total cost = £ 4436·67

Analysis

On a pro-rata basis item A will be
38% of total cost and item B, 62%

∴ $\dfrac{4436·67}{1} \times \dfrac{38}{100} = \dfrac{£1685·93}{118m^2} = £14·28/m^2$

∴ $4436·67 - 1685·93 = \dfrac{2750·74}{125m^2} = £22·01/m^2$

∴ A - £14·28/m²
  B - £22·01/m²
  C - Inc. above
  D - Inc. above

Figure 8.2   Example of operational estimating (*continued*)

Basic Data

A - Skin in commons = 118m² = 6962 bricks
B - Skin in facings = 125m² = 7375 bricks
C - Form cavity = 120m² (as work proceeds)
D - close cavity = 20m² (as work proceeds)

Labour

500 bricks (inc. waste)/day/man ~ labour
unloading and supplying materials.

$$\therefore \frac{14337}{500} = 28.67 \ (29 \text{ days}) - \text{take 30 days}$$
to include labour's and setting out.

If 2+1 gang then activities A to D carried
out in 15 days.

	£	£
∴ 2 × 8 hrs × £5·00 × 15 days =	1200	
1 × 8 hrs × £4·50 × 15 days =	540	1740·00

Materials

Commons = 6962			
+ 5% waste =	348	= 7310 at 10p =	731·00
facings = 7375			
+ 5% waste =	369	= 7744 at 18p =	1393·92
Mortar = 0·029 m³/m² × 243 m² × £42·14/m³ =			296·96
+ waste and clsg 3%			8·91
Mixing 243 × 0·029 = 7m³ × £6·24			43·68
Wall ties 3 × 243m² × 10p × (+ 10% waste)			80·20
100 bks (cav' clsg) at 10p			10·00
Total material cost =			2564·67
Total cost =			4304·67

Applied to items

On a pro-rata basis item A will be
40% of total cost and item B, 60%

A - 1721·87 = 14·59/m²
B - 2582·80 = 20·66/m²
C - Inc above
D - Inc above

Figure 8.3 Example of time and materials approach to estimating

overall time assessment to the labour and plant elements and a usage assessment against the material element. A lump sum cost is produced which can be applied to the activity descriptions if required. The analysis carried out using a time and materials approach is similar to that under the operational method, although much simplified.

Whatever approach is used, resources, labour, materials and plant must be identified under a selected method of operation. The method selected will imply a time for the activities to be carried out either based on output constants or an assessment of the overall duration which is then reduced to a time per unit of production (m, m², m³, etc.). In theory the time element implied within an estimate for an activity or a group of activities should correspond to the activity duration in both the tender programme and the contract programme derived from the tender analysis. However this will depend on a close liaison between the people producing the estimate and those producing the contract programme [23]. The method of operation selected for the estimate implies a certain level of output, and if this does not relate to the ideas upon which the contract programme is based then this deficiency may well have an effect on cost monitoring and effective cashflow management.

Analytical estimating illustrates how a selected method implies a series of output constants. Braid [24] surveyed twenty small builders who said that they approached estimate production on a time and materials basis and did not use constants. He asked them how long they would allow for hanging a flush door, including fixing of furniture. The replies varied from ½ hour to 4 ½ hours. When informed of the range of assessment, the majority said that they wanted to change their response to 2 ½ hours, thus splitting the difference. This example illustrates a very important consideration – accuracy, or perhaps more importantly, consistency.

Consider the range of cost forecasts produced by the three methods presented in Figures 8.1, 8.2 and 8.3. Each produces a different lump sum cost as follows:

Analytical approach	£6290.76
Operational approach	£4436.67
Time and materials	£4304.67

There are many reasons why estimates of the same activities under given conditions vary. As can be seen from the three analyses, the degree of detail ranges from each work element within an activity being costed to the conglomerate level whereby work elements are grouped and a time allowance made. Methods and time allowances may vary, work items can be missed or simply included as part of other elements. However, each forecast of cost, irrespective of how it has been produced, will form part of an offer to a prospective client. The successful builder will then be committed to measuring cost performance against cost forecast. Clearly then, accuracy in estimating is a misnomer, what is required is consistency in the approach adopted so that meaningful cost comparisons can be made.

Figure 8.4 illustrates the basic requirements of any adopted estimating method so that resource usage is adequately measured and costed either on an individual activity basis or on a grouped operational basis.

The important considerations will be:

(1) Identification of methods.
(2) Assessment of resource requirements in line with methods.
(3) Use of constants or assessments of time and usage to quantify resource levels.
(4) Application of a cost forecast to resource levels.
(5) Grouping of resource cost such that cost comparisons are possible.

From the above considerations it is possible to move the resource costs identified to the points in time on a contract programme where 'cost' becomes 'expenditure' and money will therefore flow out of the company. It should also be possible to monitor cost in line with the ideas presented in chapter 7, namely at selected levels – unit cost, resource cost, activity cost, operation cost – depending on the circumstances and needs.

Feedback – an essential monitoring tool

The need for consistency in a cost forecasting system was discussed earlier. This applies to all aspects of a company's financial administration systems. Consistency comes from a methodical approach to analysing the cost of an activity, and this may well be enhanced via the use of output constants selected from a company's own database.

In order to build up a level of confidence in the data used within an estimating system, some form of feedback analysis should be employed. Essentially, feedback analysis provides a medium by which actual costs are compared with estimated costs with a view to establishing the validity of the estimating process.

The use of a feedback medium has two main purposes. The first is to identify where a problem might exist, e.g. incorrect calculation of unit rates or a change in working methods. The second is to provide a data source for the setting up and operation of a database.

Any forecasting, monitoring and control medium will rely to a great

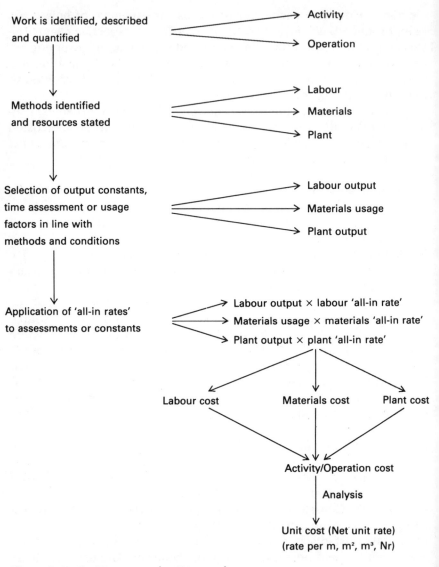

Figure 8.4 Estimate production cycle

extent on a usable database of information which must be readily available. From an estimating standpoint it is essential to be able to update historical and measured data to suit the time when the estimate is actually being made. The data must also be adjusted to relate to the specific information provided and also the form in which it is provided.

In order to make comparisons, suitable standard paperwork is required to record data collection and aid its analysis.

The ability to collect, compare and analyse cost data in a standard way is a basic essential of a cost/value reconciliation system [25]. The application and need for such systems is discussed further in chapter 11.

It is not just basic cost data and its analysis that are useful to the builder at the tender or contract stage. Cooke [2] discusses the collection and use of competing tender sums as a means of improving a company's tendering success rate.

Figure 8.5 illustrates this type of information and its collection using a standard pro-forma [16]. A company can measure the effects of making offers at various levels. This will not only apply to levels of return but also to expected cashflows.

As can be seen in Figure 8.5, the second company needs to reduce its offer by around 6% to place it first, and it would need to review the information produced on the lower half of the sheet and the reality of making such a reduction in the light of a broad view of its market opportunities.

If a database of analysed cost and possible tender levels can be maintained, then it is also possible to produce graphical representations of 'cost' and 'value' behaviour for different types of work and for given offer levels. The benefits of producing such information are discussed further in chapter 9.

Summary

The aim of this chapter was to identify the relationships which exist between estimating, the decisions taken at the estimate stage of a project, and the measurements and comparisons required within a cost monitoring system.

Documentation and the provision of information in a form which permits consistent cost forecasting is very important. The approach adopted to produce an estimate is also a critical element in the provision of reliable estimates. There appears to be little confidence in the notion of accuracy at the estimate stage, and perhaps the idea of maintaining consistency is what one should be aiming for.

The setting up of a reliable cost information database is essential if a company is to measure and monitor cost effectively at all stages in the life of a project. There are many proprietary estimating databases available, however the 'average' data provided must be related to individual company circumstances and needs. Feedback from live/ previous work is the only realistic way to set up and operate a database which will give maximum benefit.

Finally, although cost monitoring is an important aspect of the operation of a cost forecasting and control system, it is nevertheless a passive aspect. Management must have the ability to use the information provided to take appropriate decisions and effectively balance cost and value to bring about the desired conclusions.

PROJECT	Reference	MRC/6/D
Grove Estate.	Date	10/7/88

COMPARISON OF RESULTS

Tender list	Tender figure		Contract period	£ Comment	%
	Fixed	Fluct.			
1) Ball Bros.	✓		8 mths	190,000	—
2) Snode + Co	✓		"	200,000	5.26
3) Canter + Co.	✓		"	209,000	10.00
4) Dombey + Sons.	✓		"	214,000	12.26
5) Book + Co.	✓		"	215,000	13.16
6) Sneed's.	✓		"	215,500	13.42
				J.C.T '80 with	
				grants.	

ANALYSIS OF RESULT

Analysis of tender		%	Comparison of results	£	%
1	Labour	15	This company tender	209,000	
2 Main contractor's work	Plant	12	Lowest tender	190,000	
3	Material	3	Difference	19,000	10.00
4 Domestic sub-contractors		15	2nd Lowest	200,000	4.50
5 PC sums nominated sub-contractors		10	We were 3rd.		
6 PC sums nominated suppliers		3			
7 Provisional sums and contingencies		6	COMMENT Job Type :- Factory units		
8 Project overheads		12½	We were very keen to get this		
9 Firm pricing		10	contract, but as can be seen		
10 Other		1	competition was highly		
11 General overheads and profit		12½	variable. Both fluctuations and		
		100	o/h & profit were reduced by		
			5% and 2½% respectively.		

Figure 8.5 Tender comparison pro-forma

9 Cost Control

Introduction

In chapter 8, cost monitoring was put forward as an essential requirement for any forecasting and control system. However merely monitoring what has occurred is not good enough. Managers require timely, consistent information upon which to base decisions. It is a short step to relate cost forecasting and measurement to cashflow management. Examination of how cost and cashflow management should go hand in hand forms the main thrust of this chapter.

The need for consistent comparison of planned cost/cashflow against actual cost/cashflow is vital if decision-making is to be dynamic and proactive rather than merely passive and reactive.

Use of standard profiles at tender stage

There are many writers [26–30] who subscribe to the idea of an empirical approach to progress, cost, expenditure and cashflow forecasting. The methods vary from complex mathematical models to the relatively simple notion of proportionality. It is reasonable to suggest that the more complex the approach, the more it will cost to produce in terms of time and overheads. Small building companies, as in the example of the case study company, may well steer clear of the over-complex methods where a clear cost benefit from use cannot be seen. Also at the tender stage the time and money spent on producing cost/cashflow profiles will not be recovered, if the contract is not obtained. It is argued, however, that if a simple, quick and cost-effective approach is adopted, then management tender decision-making is enhanced and there will be spin-offs gained in terms of cost/cashflow management on live contracts.

Empirical evidence [26] shows that normally cost, expenditure and value on contracts will follow a common profile, that of an S-curve.

101

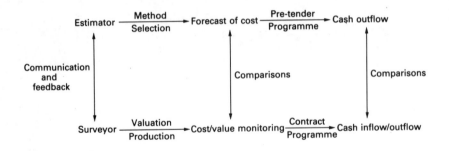

Figure 9.1   Relationship between estimating, cost control and cashflow

Evidence also suggests that contracts of the same type, e.g. schools, hospitals, etc., have similar profiles if carried out under similar conditions. Given the data collection ideas discussed in chapter 8, companies have the necessary information on which to produce standard profiles to be used as decision-making tools.

The information in example 9.1, which has been analysed from data provided by the case study company, will now be used to develop the notion of 'standard' profile production. Figure 9.1 is an overview of the relationships and data analysis required at both tender and contract stages if the above proposals are to work and also for control to be exercised.

Example   9.1

A six month school contract
Contract value (agreed final account)*   = £324 300
Contract cost (actual cost on completion)* = £282 000
Contract duration (actual = programme)   = 6 months
Retention (for example purposes only)   = 10%, with half
                                             released at
                                             practical completion,
                                             remainder at
                                             end of DLP
                                             (6 months)

Valuations monthly (payment one month later)

*Variations are not identified here, for simplicity; these are introduced and discussed in chapter 10.

Actual progress

Months	1	2	3	4	5	6
% time elapsed	17	33	50	67	83	100
% work completed (own)	5	20	40	65	90	100
% work completed (nominated sub-contractors)		5	35	70	100	
% work completed (nominated suppliers)			50	100		

Figures 9.2 to 9.5 illustrate the concept of standard profile production. The information used in Figure 9.2 has been collected and analysed using the monthly cost/value data produced after valuations on a contract (see chapter 10 for details).

Figure 9.3 shows the profiles which can be produced using the information from Figure 9.2.

Figure 9.4 shows the proportionality relationships between time, work produced, cost, value, expenditure and revenue on this contract.

Finally Figure 9.5 shows how the standard profile for this type of contract can be produced using the proportionality data. If this type of data is collected for a series of contracts of the same type, then it should be possible to produce 'standard' profiles based on the generation of 'average' profiles such as those shown in Figure 9.5.

The more the actual contract profiles used to produce a 'standard' work type profile, the better the resultant profile will be as a decision-making aid. It is also important to identify rogue contracts (contracts won in dubious circumstances, e.g. where clear mistakes were made) which may affect the reliability of profile generation.

Such profiles are also very useful as comparative reference points within the monitoring system.

Table of: (i) Monthly cost, (ii) Monthly value, (iii) Monthly cash outflow, (iv) Cashflow

Cost (£)	Months 1	2	3	4	5	6	7	8	9	10	11	12	13	Totals (£)
(a) Own work	6 250	25 000	50 000	81 250	112 500	125 000								125 000
(b) Preliminaries	1 750	7 000	14 000	22 750	31 500	35 000								35 000
(c) Dayworks	300	1 200	2 400	3 900	5 400	6 000								6 000
(d) Contingencies	750	3 000	6 000	9 750	13 500	15 000								15 000
(e) Nominated sub-contractors	—	3 250	22 750	45 500	65 000	—								65 000
(f) Nominated suppliers	—		15 000	30 000	—	—								30 000
Attendances Nominated sub-contractors			1 750	3 500	5 000	—								5 000
Nominated suppliers		250	500	1 000										1 000
Monthly cum cost	9 050	39 700	112 400	197 650	232 900	282 000								282 000
Cost	9 050	30 650	72 700	85 250	35 250	49 100								282 000
Value gross (cum)	10 407.50	45 655	129 260	227 297.50	267 835	324 300								324 300
Month value	10 407.50	35 247.50	83 605	98 037.50	40 537.50	56 465								
Net value (10% R)	9 366.75	31 722.75	75 244.5	88 233.75	36 483.75	50 818.50	50 818.50							291 870
Retention (10%)	1 040.75	3 524.75	8 360.50	9 803.75	4 053.75	5 646.50	16 215							32 430
Revenue shift	⌐	9 366.75	31 722.75	75 244.50	88 233.75	36 483.75							16 215	
Retention release							67 033.50		'No flow'					324 300
Cash outflow	5 400	25 000	72 000	90 000	47 000	42 600	(67 034) <	<	26 087	26 087	26 087	26 087 >		
Cashflow	(5 400)	(15 633)	(4 027.70)	(14 755)	(41 234)	(6 116)	(26 087)	26 087	26 087	26 087	26 087	26 087	16 215	282 000
Cum cashflow	(5 400)	(21 033)	(51 310)	(76 065)	(34 831)	(40 947)							42 302	

Figure 9.2 Summary of cost/value reconciliations

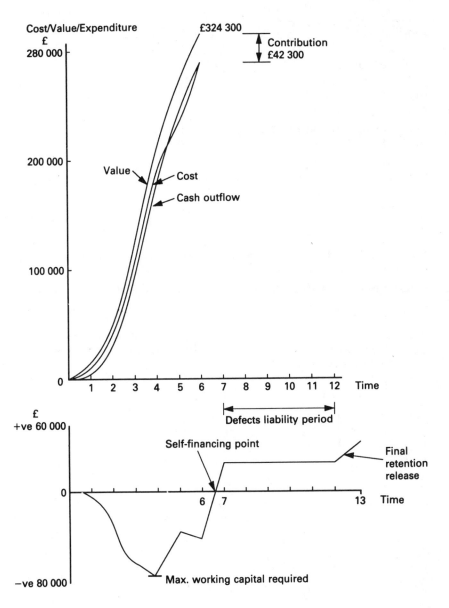

Figure 9.3   Cost/value/expenditure/cash

Months	1	2	3	4	5	6	7	13
% Time elapsed	17	33	50	67	83	100		100
% Work completed (own)	5	20	40	65	90	100		100
% Work completed (nominated sub-contractors)		5	35	70	100			
% Work completed (nominated suppliers)			50	100				
% Cost	3	14	40	70	83	100*		100
% Value	3	14	40	70	83	100*		100
% Expenditure	2	11	36	68	85	100		
% Revenue	0	3	13	36	63	74	95	100

* This will be dependent on programmed work and methods of including overheads and profit within a tender. Normally such a consistent relationship between 'cost' and 'value' would not be exhibited.

Figure 9.4 Relative progress, cost, value, expenditure and revenue positions for a contract

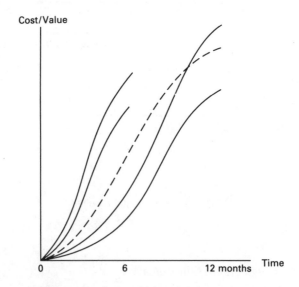

Cost/Value

0   6   12 months   Time

———— Profiles produced using database information shown in Figure 9.4

– – – – 'Standard' work type profile which can be used to produce a job-specific profile for work under consideration

Figure 9.5 Example of 'standard' profile generation

The contract budget: the first step in monitoring and control

The tender sum becomes the contract sum when a contract is awarded and the contract is signed.

If the costs/values which go to make up the contract sum are classi-fied, as described in chapter 7, and then spread across a contract programme to the points in time when they are planned to occur, effectively a contract budget is produced. It is against this contract budget that the monitoring and control procedures are set.

Figure 9.6 represents a budgeted contract programme. Actual costs of the resources employed in the various resource mixes are collected (see chapter 10 for details) using standard allocation/usage sheets, and comparison of actual against planned costs takes place within the medium of a cost/value reconciliation. The next logical step in the control process is the production of a cashflow statement.

Production of a contract cashflow statement

The budgeted programme (Figure 9.6) identifies the points at which cost is incurred and value measured. Figure 9.7 depicts the 'cost' and 'value' curves which, as can be seen (see chapter 10), can also be used as reference points whereby actual cost and value profiles can be plotted to aid the measurement of variances.

The next step is to identify the individual resource costs and then to shift these to the points at which outflow of money is likely to occur (expenditure points). Two approaches to identifying these expenditure points can be adopted to suit particular needs. Cooke and Jepson [26] describe a weighted average approach to this exercise, for example:

Labour – payment delay	= 1 week
Materials – payment delay	= 4 weeks from invoice date (8 weeks)
Plant – payment delay	= 4 weeks from invoice date (8 weeks)
Sub-contractors – payment delay	= 2 weeks from application (6 weeks)

Using analysis of the estimate in question will provide the propor-tions of each resource compared with total cost as follows:

Labour	26%
Materials	28%
Plant	9%
Sub-contractors	37%

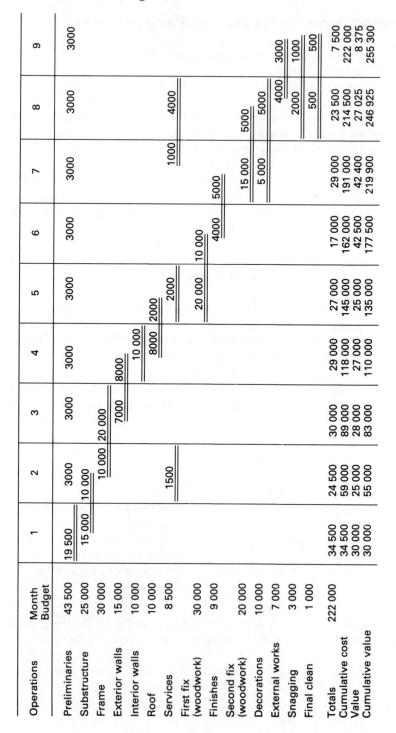

Operations	Month Budget	1	2	3	4	5	6	7	8	9
Preliminaries	43 500	19 500	3000	3000	3000	3000	3000	3000	3000	3000
Substructure	25 000	15 000	10 000								
Frame	30 000		10 000	20 000							
Exterior walls	15 000			7000	8000						
Interior walls	10 000				10 000						
Roof	10 000				8000	2000					
Services	8 500		1500			2000		1000		
First fix (woodwork)	30 000					20 000	10 000				
Finishes	9 000						4000	5000			
Second fix (woodwork)	20 000							15 000	5000		
Decorations	10 000							5 000	5000		
External works	7 000								4000	3000
Snagging	3 000								2000	1000
Final clean	1 000								500	500
Totals	222 000	34 500	24 500	30 000	29 000	27 000	17 000	29 000	23 500	7 500
Cumulative cost		34 500	59 000	89 000	118 000	145 000	162 000	191 000	214 500	222 000
Value		30 000	25 000	28 000	27 000	25 000	42 500	42 400	27 025	8 375
Cumulative value		30 000	55 000	83 000	110 000	135 000	177 500	219 900	246 925	255 300

Figure 9.6 Budgeted contract programme

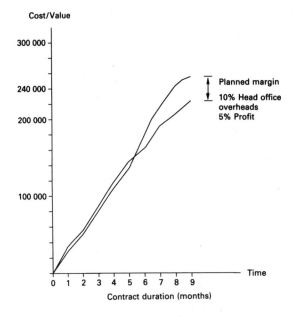

Figure 9.7 Planned 'cost' and 'value' profiles

The weighted average delay in making payments can be calculated as follows:

Labour = 1 × 26% = 0.26 week
Materials = 8 × 28% = 2.24 weeks
Plant = 8 × 9% = 0.72 week
Sub-contractors = 6 × 37% = 2.22 weeks
5.44 weeks

In this case 5 weeks would be used as an expenditure point, which is the point at which costs incurred at the end of week 4 will become a cash outflow at the end of week 9.

The alternative is to analyse the expenditure pattern for each resource and use this to produce a more accurate total expenditure profile. Figure 9.8 represents this approach.

The normal expenditure patterns for each resource is:

(1) Labour receives wages at the end of the first week's work.
(2) Materials are required to be paid for 28 days after the invoice date in order to receive the cash discount for prompt payment.

Therefore, if an invoice is received at the end of month 1, payment should be made before the end of month 2, giving a possible 8-week credit period.

(3) Plant is normally treated in a similar way to materials.

(4) Sub-contractors may well be a problem. While it might be beneficial to set up a sub-contract agreement which allows for a sub-contractor to be paid when a builder receives payment, this will of course affect the sub-contractor's cashflow management. It has become usual in recent years for labour-only sub-contractors to receive payments on a weekly basis, and for labour-and-materials sub-contractors to make applications every two weeks for payment two weeks later. In the example which follows, applications are made every four weeks, a company certificate is prepared (see chapter 6) and payment is made two weeks after this certificate has been prepared, making a 6-week delay period. Whichever approach is adopted, it is very important to seek a clear agreement, at the outset, and then maintain this agreement to the mutual benefit of both parties.

Value is converted into revenue by shifting monthly values to the point at which monies are received (cash inflow). Normally, if a standard form of building contract is used, this will occur 14 days after certification. Certification should take place 7 days from the valuation date (JCT 1980 [31] and IFC 1984 [32] state that the architect should issue a certificate within seven days of a valuation). In this example, value is converted into revenue by a shift to the end of month 2 and by subtracting retention of 5%.

Figure 9.8 shows how resource costs can be shifted in time to the points at which they become expenditure, and how value is shifted to the point at which it becomes revenue. Actual cost, value and cashflow can also be plotted on this schedule as part of the monitoring and control exercise. Figure 9.9 presents the forecasted cashflow profile for the same contract. Again the actual cashflow can be compared graphically with the estimated cashflows.

Summary

Building on the basic idea of cost monitoring, cost control should be seen essentially as a decision-making tool.

Control commences at the tender stage, when cost and value targets are established. The use of standard cost/cashflow profiles at the tender stage as decision-making aids is recommended; these can then be used to assist future decisions about tendering for various types of contract in line with working capital availability and notional cashflow generation.

Months	1	2	3	4	5	6	7	8	9	10	11	12	13	14	15	Totals
Cost																
Cumulative cost	34 500	59 000	89 000	118 000	145 000	162 000	191 000	214 000	222 000							
Cumulative labour cost	8 970	15 340	23 140	30 680	37 700	42 120	49 660	55 648	58 450	58 450						58 450
Cumulative materials cost	9 660	16 520	24 920	33 040	40 600	45 360	53 480	59 920	62 800	62 800						62 800
Cumulative plant cost	4 778	8 056	9 655	11 254	12 853	14 452	16 051	17 650	19 750	19 750						19 750
Cumulative sub-contractor cost	1 000	5 000	11 000	13 000	33 000	43 000	63 000	77 000	81 000	81 000						81 000
Labour expenditure	8 970	15 340	23 140	30 680	37 700	42 120	49 660	55 648	58 450	58 450						
Materials expenditure	—	9 660	16 520	24 920	33 040	40 600	45 360	53 480	59 920	62 800						
Plant expenditure	—	4 778	8 056	9 655	11 254	12 853	14 452	16 051	17 650	19 750						
Sub-contractor expenditure	—	1 000	5 000	11 000	13 000	33 000	43 000	63 000	77 000	81 000						
Cumulative expenditure	8 970	30 778	52 716	76 255	94 994	128 573	152 472	188 179	213 020	222 000						
Cumulative value	30 000	55 000	83 000	110 000	135 000	177 500	219 900	246 925	255 300							
Cumulative retention	1 500	2 750	4 150	5 500	6 750	8 875	10 995	12 346	12 765							
Net value	28 500	52 250	78 850	104 500	128 250	168 625	208 905	234 579	242 535							
Revenue		28 500	52 250	78 850	104 500	128 250	168 625	208 905	234 579	242 535	242 535 <		'No flow'		> 248 918	248 918
Retention release }											6 383		Retention release		6 382	6 382
											248 918				255 300	
Cumulative cashflow	(8 970)	(2 278)	(466)	2 595	9 506	(323)	16 153	20 726	21 559	26 918	26 918	26 918	26 918	26 918	26 918	33 300

Figure 9.8   Cashflow statement

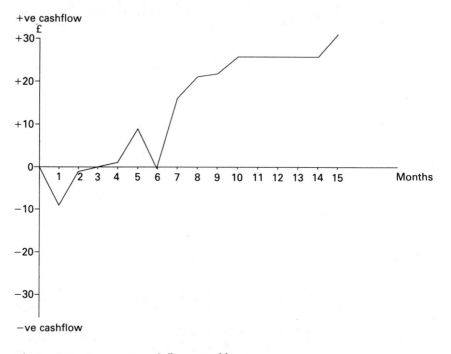

Figure 9.9   Forecast cashflow profile

Two examples of how cost and cashflow analyses can be produced, one using a weighted average to identify outflows of money and the other using actual outflow points, are given. The approach chosen will probably be governed by the level of accuracy/consistency desired by the user.

The production of a budgeted programme is the first step in the contract control cycle. From this budget a contract cashflow statement can be produced, against which both actual cost and actual cashflow can be monitored. All important variances (positive and negative) are considered in relation to the control and decision-making process.

10 Resource Cost Management and Cashflow

Introduction

Cashflow budgeting, monitoring and control are a natural progression from the procedures examined in earlier chapters.

Cash, while being a resource in its own right, is also the means by which other resources are acquired.

The provision of cash in the desired amounts, and at the right time, is one of the most important aspects of managing a construction company.

The need for a system which allows the cash needs and timing on contracts to be identified will be examined.

The ingredients of a cost/value reconciliation system have been identified in chapter 9 and it is vital that comparisons are also made in respect of planned cashflow and actual cashflow, since these are the key to profit/loss reporting.

The need to provide timely, consistent information to managers will again be an underlying theme.

Concept of returns on contract investment

Every contract carried out by a building company requires an initial investment which will not be recovered until sometime in the future. Two of the factors which cause funds to be 'locked up' on contracts are stage payments and, in a greater number of cases, disagreements. In the latter case it is only when there is a meeting of minds that monies are released, and in the former case the contract sets the pattern for inflow so long as the work has been carried out and is efficiently valued. There are many other reasons for builders receiving monies late, for example under-valuation quite often occurs as a result of mistakes on the part of both the client's representatives and the builder. However the important aspect for the contractor to consider is: will a profit be made at the end of the day, and is that profit in line with the profitability anticipated at the time the tender was prepared?

If the factors affecting the receipt of monies are classified as variables, then they can be considered under the following classifications:

(1) Within the control of the builder (varying degrees of control).
(2) Outside the builder's control

Such things as labour strength, sub-contractor performance and under- or over-valuation are, to a greater or lesser extent, within the contractor's control. However, client delays and architect's variations are outside the contractor's control and are difficult and in some cases impossible to anticipate, let alone control.

Such variables on contracts not only affect profit but also profitability.

Profit is quite simply the difference between the total income (value) of a contract and the total cost (actual cost) at the end of a job (i.e. the agreed final account when all payments have been made and received). Profitability, however, is the rate of making a profit in relation to the builder's investment. Quite often it is the maintenance of profitability which is overlooked, in the pursuit of increased turnover through reduced margins, even though profitability and the actual receipt of monies is where long-term stability is achieved.

It is also important to remember that the measurement and maintenance of profitability is fundamental to a company's corporate planning and monitoring activities, with 'returns on capital employed' (invested) being a key factor in whether or not a company can be considered to be financially successful.

There are three distinct areas which affect a company's profitability:

(1) The company's desired 'return on capital employed' (ROCE) and its ability to maintain 'market share'.
(2) The mark-up on contract costs required to achieve the desired ROCE and its effect on tender success rates.
(3) The real cost of 'variables' to maintain profitability.

Consider the following example. A small builder commences work on a contract worth £110 000 and lasting one year. His margin on costs (direct and indirect) is 10% and he is paid in full on contract completion by the purchaser of a factory unit which forms the speculative development.

Therefore the value of work
(received in one year)   = £110 000 (future value)
The cost of work
(over the contract period)   = £100 000 (present value)
Time period   = 1 year
Margin (interest rate)   = 10% p.a.

This situation can be represented graphically as follows:

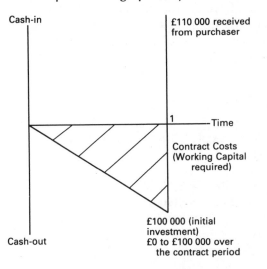

Even though the £100 000 will be expended in varying amounts over the contract period, the reality of the situation is that this sum is committed to this contract from the outset, and thus part or all of this investment cannot be realistically invested in other projects and certainly not without careful planning.

In effect it is 'locked up' in this contract, and ROCE is not achieved until completion.

What will happen if the purchaser (client) delays payment for a year? The resultant cash flow would appear thus:

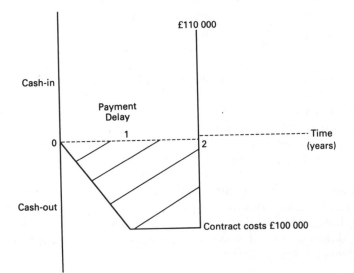

The builder will still make 10% profit on the initial investment, but profitability will have decreased because the time period for receipt of monies has increased. For example, if an investment of £100 000 is now required to give a return of £110 000 in 2 years' time, the compound interest formula

$$PV = \frac{FV}{(1 + i)^n}$$

can be used to calculate the profitability as a result of the payment delay. Therefore

Present value (PV) = £100 000
Future value (FV) = £110 000
Period (n) = 2 years
Profitability = i

Therefore

$$100\ 000 = \frac{110\ 000}{(1 + i)^2}$$

and $i = 0.049$ or 4.9% compound p.a.

This means that this company's profitability has been reduced from 10% p.a. to 4.9% p.a. compound over two years, because of the delay in payment.

This simple example demonstrates that if a company merely measures profit, then it is only measuring the size of cash flows (inflow–outflow), whereas the measurement of profitability will take into account both the amount and time of cashflows, and this leads to consideration of returns on investment.

However, a company operating under the traditional competitive tendering arrangement, employing a standard form of building contract (JCT), faces numerous inflows and outflows of cash because of the stage payment facility (normally monthly) of the main contract and the varying payment requirements of suppliers and sub-contractors. Each valuation and certification point will represent a large inflow of cash (less retention monies) while payments throughout the month for sub-contractors, suppliers and wages represent outflows. The diagram on page 117 represents this often highly complex situation.

As can be seen from the diagram, the resultant number of outflows and inflows, all occurring at different points in time, requires a builder to fund the contract up to a self-financing point. This gives rise to three problems for the builder:

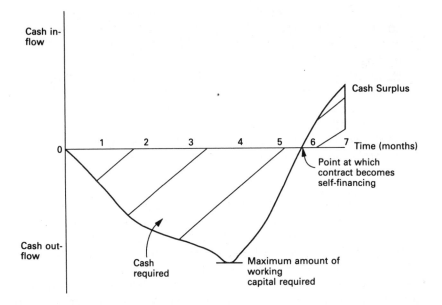

(1) Forecasting when the contract becomes self-financing.
(2) Funding the job in the light of stage payments.
(3) Measurement of ROCE.

Chapter 9 showed how a contract cashflow statement could be produced whereby a contracts self-financing point, its funding needs and ROCE can be identified.

Each contract cashflow budget will constitute a major element of company cashflow.

Relationship between contract cashflow and company cashflow

The majority of cashflows experienced by a small builder occur as a result of the contractual and credit arrangements existing on a series of contracts in any trading period.

Company cashflow represents a series of aggregated cashflows generated by contracts which are then added to head office cashflows as a result of:

(1) Head office expenditure – expenditure can be identified within a company's accounts by items such as rent, rates, interest charges, telephones charges, office equipment hire charges, payments to shareholders, tax, directors' fees, salaries, etc. These items are recorded in the accounts on an accruals basis, that is to say they are entered when incurred, at the time of an invoice or time of

occurrence, not when cash is paid out. Therefore as with costs on contracts, head office costs will need to be allocated to the time when money is expended in order to evaluate expenditure over a trading period.

(2) Head office income – income will be derived from selling head office services, the majority of which will come from the contributions each contract makes to company overheads. Any surplus of income after all of the liabilities are taken care of will be the gross profit margin, which can then be related to the capital employed to generate turnover. It is from this relationship that ROCE is derived [33].

The review period for either budget preparation or performance measurement is likely to be a trading year. In any trading year a small general building company will carry out a variety of sizes and types of contracts, each starting at different points in time with some finishing and achieving final account agreement in a new trading period. What is therefore required is a rolling approach to cashflow budgeting and monitoring whereby figures (e.g. outstanding work-in-progress, retention releases, etc.) are brought forward and represented in the trading period in which they are likely to occur.

1986
Profit Statement

	£
Turnover	1 030 311.00
Less:	
Production costs	865 319.00
Profit on direct costs (Gross profit)	164 992.00
Less:	
Administration expenses (Overheads)	123 176.00
Net profit before tax and interest	41 816.00

$$\therefore \text{Profit} = \frac{41\ 816}{1\ 030\ 311} = 4.1\% \text{ of sales}$$

Figure 10.1 Typical profit statement

Integration, cashflow and accounting systems

In chapter 7, Figure 7.4 was presented to illustrate the basic links between accounting information used in different company accounting systems at various levels.

The idea that common financial data are put to different uses within a company's management and financial accounting systems was also identified in earlier chapters.

Examples of how the case study company's profit or trading account might be presented, firstly in financial accounting format, and then in management accounting style, illustrate this notion. In Figure 10.1, the traditional profit statement identifies if an overall profit or loss has been achieved during a trading period, whereas the management account approach using the same common data (Figure 10.2) identifies specific contract profit/loss and also the individual contributions made to the overhead and profit fund. The data used in Figure 10.2 are extracted from the summarised final cost/value reconciliations for contracts in hand [25].

Jones [34] comments that chartered accountants appear to misunderstand the concept of integrated accounting procedures, and he attempts to clarify the situation by producing the following set of rules:

(1) All costs are posted to a work-in-progress control account in the nominal ledger.
(2) They remain in the nominal ledger until positively removed, at the time when a complete and final invoice is rendered to the client, when:
    (a) Cost of sales account is debited.
    (b) Work-in-progress account is credited.
    'Work-in-progress' takes on a new and more significant meaning:
    (c) It is a positive amount which can be changed only by double entry.
(3) No cost sheet can be removed by accident or design without the fact becoming known.
(4) The effect will be to have more reliable trading account information.

The linking and integration of the two systems (financial and management accounting) improves the reporting function and clearly aids management's decision-making capabilities.

Figure 10.3 illustrates how cost, management and financial accounts can be interrelated and integrated.

It has not been an objective of this book to relate the use of computers to the running of accounting systems. A key aim has been the discussion of the benefits of systemisation, and if a good set of principles can be laid down then a good suite of computer programs

Contract/Work types	1	2	3	4	5	6	7	8	9	Jobbing work	Total
Production costs	98 117	59 040	94 481	152 447	57 252	161 929	103 230	34 850	45 240	58 733	865 319
Administration expenses	18 024	12 960	15 519	9 253	16 148	14 771	16 830	7 216	7 000	5 455	123 176
Total cost	116 141	72 000	110 000	161 700	73 400	176 700	120 060	42 066	52 240	64 188	988 495
Turnover	125 000	75 500	110 500	163 700	75 300	175 600	133 400	41 000	52 000	78 311	1 030 311
Profit	8 859	3 500	500	2 000	1 900		13 340			14 123	41 816
Loss						1 100		1 066	240		
Margin (%)	7.1	4.6	0.5	1	2.5	(0.6)	10	(2)	(0.5)	18	4.1

Note: all figures (except margin) are in £s.

Figure 10.2 Typical management account profit summary

A flowchart to show how cost, management and financial accounts should be interrelated and integrated

Time Book	Wages sheet		Cash	Nominal ledger accounts	Job cost ledger
	Payroll + Analysis			Wages Overheads Service dept Construction in progress	Wage cost
Salary list	Payroll + Analysis			Salaries Overheads Service dept Construction in progress	Salaries cost
Material & Plant Order Delivery note Invoices	Materials received book			Purchases Overheads Service dept Construction in progress	Materials cost
Sub-contract Order Application	Valuation			Sub-contract Construction in progress	Sub-contract cost
Internal charges	Analysis			Departments Overheads Construction in progress	Internal charges
Gross applications	Certificates			Progress payments Retentions	

Figure 10.3 Integrated accounts [after Padget P., *Accounting in the Construction Industry*, Institute of Cost and Management Accountants, 1983]

can be produced which will allow data relationships and integration across estimating, cost control and accounting procedures to occur.

Relationship between resource control and cashflow

The contract cashflow statement, identified earlier, demonstrated how the main resource items are related to cost incurred and subsequent outflow of monies.

The main resource items are:

1. Labour
2. Materials
3. Plant
4. Sub-contractors (labour only/labour and materials)

Each resource element cost will be analysed within a separate sub-system of both the financial and management accounts. Figures 10.4 to 10.7 examine how these sub-systems should operate.

Figure 10.4 illustrates the way in which integration might take place within the labour accounting system. Three key points at which cash outflow occurs are identified.

Amounts of cash outflow to labour are shown on payslips and the times at which flows occur are recorded by cash vouchers, which are either processed by the company or a security company employed to organise wages payments (many companies employ the services of security companies to operate their wages systems). Clearance accounts identify the amounts and times of payments to statutory bodies (PAYE, National Insurance, etc.).

Figure 10.5 presents the same concept with materials in mind. The raising of a cash voucher again identifies the outflow point with the agreed invoice amount identifying the expenditure level.

Figure 10.6 represents the accounting sub-systems for plant. As with the previous system, it is the cash voucher position which identifies cash outflow.

Finally, the sub-contracting sub-systems are illustrated in Figure 10.7. In this case it is the payment certificate which identifies both the amount and the point at which outflow occurs.

Cash inflow element

As work is carried out, not only has cost and expenditure to be controlled, but value and revenue must be measured and compared with cost/expenditure in order that financial performance can be evaluated. The point at which valuations occur on contracts is either set out in the

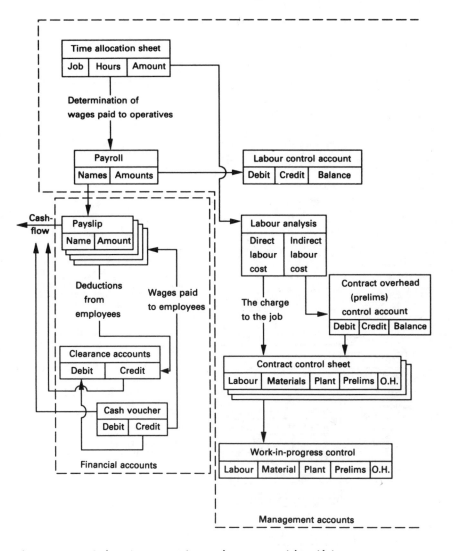

Figure 10.4 Labour accounting sub-systems identifying documentation [after Thornton N., *Management Accounting*, Heinemann, 1978]

contract or established by agreement with the client. The same will also be true for certificate, payment and retention levels. The level of revenue and the point of inflow is set out and will occur at a predetermined date after certification (e.g. JCT 1980 80 [31] – inflow = 14 days after certificate).

Before going on to review how the valuation and payment system might operate, it is worth recounting some of the main problems

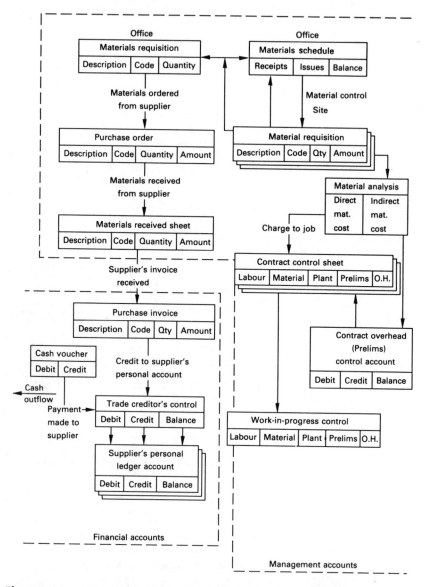

Figure 10.5 Materials accounting sub-systems identifying documentation [after Thornton, *Management Accounting*]

associated with valuation procedures:

(1) Accurate measurement and recording of the work carried out.
(2) Agreement with the client or client's representatives as to the value of the work as priced and then carried out.

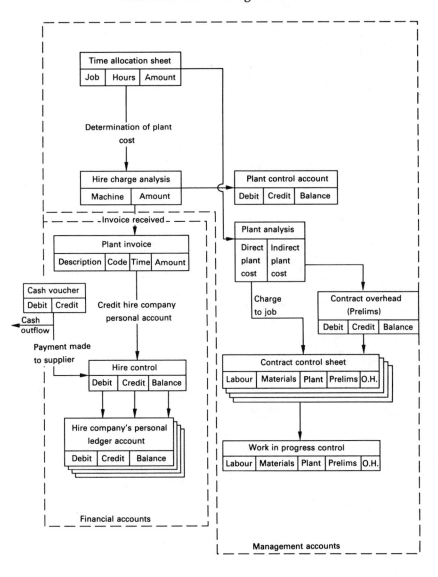

Figure 10.6 Plant accounting sub-systems identifying documentation [after Thornton, *Management Accounting*]

(3) The identification and control of under- or over-valuation of the work and the possible consequences of such occurrences.

(4) The accurate and consistent comparison of the value as measured with the cost as incurred with the reconciliation system.

(5) The identification of 'late' payments, measuring the consequences and the instigation of suitable corrective measures.

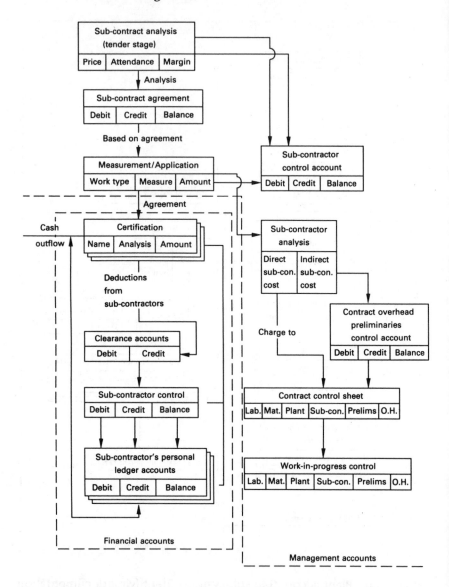

Figure 10.7 Sub-contractor accounting sub-systems identifying documentation [after Thornton, *Management Accounting*]

These five factors are investigated further in chapter 11.

Finally, Figure 10.8 represents the valuation and payment accounting sub-systems. The certificate (invoice) identifies the amount of revenue to flow in, and this will occur either within an agreed period or later in the case of delinquent clients.

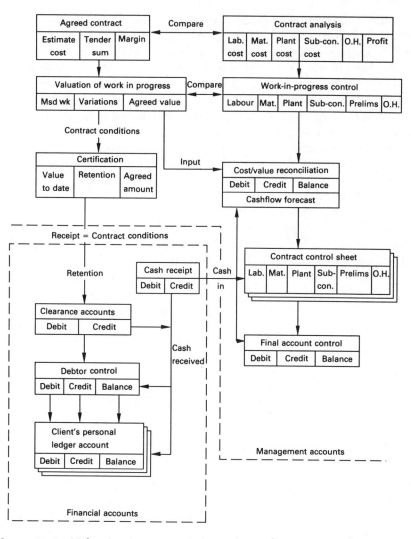

Figure 10.8   Valuation/payment accounting sub-systems [after Thornton, *Management Accounting*]

Summary

The primary objective of this chapter was to investigate how resource costs become cash outflows, and how these might be related to values which become cash inflows.

It is from these relationships that comparisons are made which allow monitoring to take place, then control and finally cashflow budgets to be produced for the future.

More important than measuring profit is the measurement of cash-flow, and from this profitability. Also highlighted are the variables which are likely to affect cashflow and thus profitability on contracts.

The key issues of identifying when contracts become self-financing, funding up to this point and measurement of ROCE are central to management's ability to manage contract finances.

Contract cashflows, when aggregated and added to head office cash-flows, become company cashflow.

The data presented in financial statements are not a very useful management tool, in contrast to the information format used in management accounts. The ability to use common financial data through-out a control and monitoring system must improve the usefulness of accounting information for management purposes.

This theme of integration within the control process is illustrated in the analysis of the resource cash outflow sub-systems and the valuation/payment cash inflow and reconciliation sub-systems, which should form the central core of a company's accounting procedures.

11 An Integrated Model Financial Control System

Introduction

A company's final set of trading statements, in the form of a balance sheet, profit statement, and sources and application of funds flow statement, represent its financial status at the end of a trading period.

While these statements can be said to be relatively true only at the moment in time they are drawn up, they are nevertheless the culmination of a large number of transactions which have occurred during the past year.

These transactions can be considered as identifying inflows and outflows of cash at times specified by various contractual arrangements. Thus the final statements will represent how money has been spent, monies due to flow out and into the company shortly, and the relative returns on the capital invested in various contracts.

A company which has been trading for a number of years will have a series of end-of-year statements which can be said to form a database of financial performance information.

Depending on the level of consistency apparent within the final statements [35], the data presented can be analysed and developed for use in a forecasting, monitoring and control system. Such a system allows a set of financial targets to be established for the next trading year. These targets can then be used by management as a means of comparing actual against planned performance. Any deviations from a corporate financial plan can also be reconciled on a regular basis.

During a research project, Canter [1] selected and reviewed the accounts of twelve small building companies with a view to examining the attributes required in a financial management information system. One of the objectives of this examination was to evaluate the level of consistency in both data presentation and performance measurement. If clear performance trends can be extracted from a company's accounts, such trends can be used as the basis for establishing the targeting medium.

A commercial spreadsheet package [36] was used to present the financial data in a convenient form and then to analyse the data in a structured fashion. A company's balance sheet and profit statement data are input for a five year period and traditional ratio analysis [37,38] used to highlight the financial trends. It must be emphasised that the use of ratio analysis as a performance-indicating medium is fraught with danger [17] and great care must be exercised in the selection of individual ratios, and perhaps more importantly how they are used.

The data analysis which follows is based on an actual company's accounts, the case study company referred to throughout this book.

Finally, the attributes of a model system are discussed. Taking a previous year's financial performance, performance targets for a future year are set, against which management decisions can be taken. Then a set of final statements form the basis of an on-going financial management process.

The basis of model system design

The majority of small building companies operate in multi-product/ service markets, as was shown in chapter 2. It would therefore be beneficial to identify the most lucrative markets to continue to operate in, and reflect such market orientation within the overall corporate strategy.

It can be argued that companies of similar size and operating in confined markets encounter similar production costs levels on contracts of similar type (see chapter 2). From this it seems reasonable to theorise that competition between such companies is largely based on administration costs and desired profit margins. If this is the case then it seems reasonable to assume that companies who are able to monitor and control company costs realistically are likely to enjoy a competitive edge over their rivals.

A key aspect of any financial modelling system is the ability to extract financial trends from previous trading periods as depicted in the accounts, and use these trends to develop forecasts and targets for future periods.

Research has shown [1] that for companies carrying out workloads consisting of contracts which do not vary much in nature from period to period, a high level of consistency exists in the relationship between turnover, production and administration costs. The relationship between these three factors is a good reference point for a company's corporate budgeting exercises.

The accounts used in this chapter belong to a real company (case study company) and the first step will be to analyse the data in these accounts to establish the trends needed to develop the targets required to be established within the model system.

The first target required to be established within the corporate budget is the desired return on capital employed. Once a desired return on capital employed (ROCE) target has been established, the next step is to evaluate how much working capital the company requires at a given turnover level.

The relationship between profit, profitability and cashflow was discussed in chapter 10, and this relationship will be used to produce a forecast balance sheet, profit statement and management ratios.

There is clearly a need to finance work adequately, and to be able to measure the cost consequences of such finance and the eventual contribution that contracts make to overheads and profit. Trend analysis identifies finance requirements, cost consequences and returns from contracts, from which targets can again be established.

The idea of using a system of control responsibility levels was introduced in chapter 7 and this idea is employed within the corporate budget so that a series of management budgets can be produced for monitoring and control purposes.

Accounts analysis – the first step

Figures 11.1, 11.2 and 11.3 represent the profit and loss statement, balance sheet and ratio analysis data for a five year period for the case study company.

A general commentary on the five year financial performance follows which demonstrates the ability to identify a series of trends. Also employed to amplify the commentary are Figures 11.4 to 11.7 which are referred to when necessary.

A commercial management software package incorporating an integrated spreadsheet, graphics, database and word-processing facilities was used to generate this information.

As can be clearly identified from the accounts and Figure 11.4, turnover increased by significant margins in each of the five years under consideration. The increases can be represented by at least two £100 000 contracts being added to the books in each trading year. Increases in turnover of this magnitude not only have financing implications but also administrative consequences, both of which require careful consideration.

The accounts show that the provision of capital has come from a 100% increase in share capital, large increases in loan facilities (67% in 1984/85) and a heavier dependence on overdraft facility for short-term funding needs (86% increase in both 1984 and 1985).

Company Comparisons Pro-forma

Profit & Loss

COMPANY NAME: 'I' Ltd

Item	A 1985	B 1984	C 1983	D 1982	E 1981
Turnover	1 077 459.00	842 255.00	504 296.00	393 996.00	154 683.00
Change %	27.93	67.02	28.00	154.71	—
Production costs	841 887.00	675 757.00	377 025.00	283 513.00	113 881.00
Change %	24.58	79.23	32.98	148.96	—
Admin. expenses	181 464.00	137 976.00	116 133.00	96 150.00	31 133.00
Change %	31.52	18.81	20.78	208.84	—
Interest received & similar income	219.00	85.00	0.00	0.00	0.00
Change %	157.65	—	0.00	0.00	—
Net profit before tax & interest	31 991.00	15 687.00	11 138.00	14 333.00	−2 409.00
Change %	103.93	40.84	−22.29	694.98	—
Interest paid/Pref. div.	22 336.00	12 920.00	6 336.00	6 880.00	0.00
Depreciation	0.00	0.00	0.00	0.00	0.00
Change %	0.00	0.00	0.00	0.00	—
Taxation	3 700.00	−3 615.00	−1 650.00	5 000.00	−1 258.00
Transfer (to) from Deferred tax	0.00	0.00	0.00	0.00	−13 464.00
Net profit after tax & interest	28 291.00	19 302.00	6 452.00	2 453.00	−1 151.00
Change %	46.57	199.16	163.02	313.12	—

Figure 11.1   Profit & loss statement

Ref.: 'I'

BALANCE SHEET

ITEM	1985	1984	1983	1982	1981
Fixed assets (net)	213 084.00	141 260.00	116 558.00	49 746.00	40 929.00
Change %	50.85	21.19	134.31	21.54	—
Current assets					
Stock	7 174.00	10 741.00	3 000.00	2 000.00	2 000.00
Change %	−33.21	258.03	50.00	0.00	—
Work in progress	67 290.00	59 960.00	51 000.00	52 250.00	51 164.00
Change %	12.22	17.57	−2.39	2.12	—
Debtors	234 581.00	121 656.00	70 525.00	73 011.00	32 342.00
Change.%	92.82	72.50	−3.40	125.75	—
Cash at bank & on deposit	1 840.00	10 947.00	113.00	70.00	37.00
Change %	−83.19	9 587.61	61.43	89.19	—
Corporation tax	0.00	0.00	0.00	0.00	0.00
Change %	0.00	0.00	0.00	0.00	0.00

BALANCE SHEET *continued*

ITEM	1985	1984	1983	1982	1981
Current assets total	310 885.00	203.304.00	124 638.00	127 331.00	85 543.00
Change %	52.92	63.12	−2.11	48.85	—
Total assets	523 969.00	344 564.00	241 196.00	177 077.00	126 472.00
Change %	52.07	42.86	36.21	40.01	—
Current liabilities					
Creditors	210 864.00	154 336.00	108 424.00	81 356.00	43 389.00
Change %	36.63	42.34	33.27	87.50	—
Overdraft	96 579.00	51 737.00	27 680.00	39 934.00	44 634.00
Change %	86.67	86.91	−30.69	−10.53	—
Taxation	42 145.00	22 224.00	11 100.00	7 658.00	1 040.00
Change %	89.64	100.22	44.95	636.35	—
Dividend	0.00	0.00	0.00	0.00	—
Change %	0.00	0.00	0.00	—	—
Net current assets	−38 703.00	−24 993.00	−22 566.00	−1 617.00	−3 520.00
Capital employed	174 381.00	116 267.00	93 992.00	48 129.00	37 409.00
Financed by:					
Share capital	32 080.00	32 080.00	32 080.00	16 040.00	16 040.00
Change %	0.00	0.00	100.00	0.00	—
Reserves	56 497.00	34 787.00	14 234.00	23 822.00	21 369.00
Change %	62.41	144.39	−40.25	11.48	—
Loans	74 038.00	44 214.00	47 678.00	8 267.00	0.00
Change %	67.45	−7.27	476.73	—	—
Preference Shares/ Debenture	11 766.00	5 186.00	0.00	0.00	—
Change %	126.88	—	0.00	—	—
Funds employed	174 381.00	116 267.00	93 992.00	48 129.00	37 409.00
Number of ordinary shares	32 080.00	32 080.00	32 080.00	16 040.00	16 040.00
Number of employees (admin. & production)	19.00	17.00	15.00	15.00	15.00

Figure 11.2   Balance sheet

Ref.: 'I'	1985	1984	1983	1982	1981
Ratio Analysis					
Overall Performance					
ROCE (shareholders)	36.12	23.46	24.05	35.96	−6.44
ROCE (total)	18.35	13.49	11.85	29.78	−6.44
PBTI/Turnover	2.97	1.86	2.21	3.64	−1.56
Turnover/Share capital & reserves	12.16	12.60	10.89	9.88	4.13
Turnover/Funds employed	6.18	7.24	5.37	8.19	4.13
Solvency					
Capital owned/Capital employed × 100	50.80	57.51	49.27	82.82	100.00
PBTI/Fixed interest payments	1.43	1.21	1.76	2.08	—
Liquidity					
Current ratio	0.89	0.89	0.85	0.99	0.96
Acid test	0.68	0.58	0.48	0.57	0.36
Debtor days	79.47	52.72	51.04	67.64	76.32
Creditor days	71.43	66.88	78.48	75.37	102.38
C.A./F.A.	1.46	1.44	1.07	2.56	2.09
Market tests					
ROE	31.94	28.87	13.93	6.15	−3.08
Earnings/share	88.19	60.17	20.11	15.29	−7.18
Dividend cover	—	—	—	—	—
Other ratios					
Stock days	2.43	4.65	2.17	1.85	4.72
Turnover/Number of employees	56 708.37	49 544.41	33 619.73	26 266.40	10 312.20

Figure 11.3 Ratio analysis

Research has identified [1] a clear proportional relationship between turnover, direct costs of construction and general overheads, given a reasonably mixed general workload.

In the case study instance, a turnover increase of 154% in 1982 resulted in administration expenses (overheads) increasing by 208%. It is difficult to measure how much administration will cost at any given turnover level. Whether in fact a 208% increase in overhead costs was

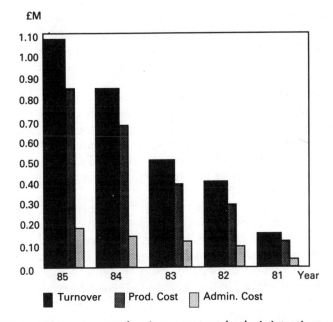

Figure 11.4 Turnover, production costs and administration costs for company 'I'

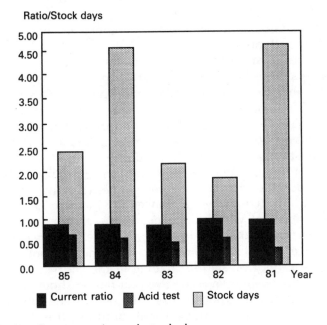

Figure 11.5 Current ratio and stock days

warranted cannot be commented on. What can be said is that, having increased the administrative facility, which is implied by the cost increase, in 1982, overheads rose from this new level steadily and remained a consistent proportion of turnover thereafter (see Figure 11.4).

It is important to establish the point at which major changes in overhead levels, in line with turnover movements, are necessary. The cost consequences of trying to administer workloads beyond current capabilities can be dangerous. It is very important to attempt to identify the physical administration needs, dictated by type of work and workload, to quantify these in terms of personnel and equipment, and then to apply a cost to them.

Research has again demonstrated [1] that, provided the types of work carried out by a company do not change drastically, then as turnover fluctuates, administration costs move in a relatively consistent manner and can be measured as a constant proportion of turnover. The same behaviour was exhibited by production costs: as turnover increased, production costs moved in line with and remained a consistent proportion of turnover.

Such relationships are essential if forecasting of alternative financial strategies is to be achieved with any degree of confidence.

The sources of capital required to generate turnover were identified previously. The result of the various funding methods adopted has been a movement away from being a lowly geared company (relying mainly on shareholder funding) to much higher levels of gearing (more use of borrowed money).

The composite situation of increased turnover, high gearing and shareholder's funds being 'turned over' at an increasing rate demonstrates the principle of 'leverage' [39] very graphically. Shareholders are benefiting from enhanced returns on their capital investment in line with their share of the profits achieved on turnover. It is interesting to note that this occurs despite the very slim profit margins. This indicates that the most important factor in producing a return on capital employed might well be the number of times share capital can be turned over or used, rather than the final margin between 'cost' and 'value'.

To sum up, this company has managed to increase turnover over a five year period, well within capital provisions, and as such can be said to be comfortably trading within its means in the medium to long term. The objective is to plan to continue to trade in this manner.

The same cannot be said for trading in the short term. The company's liquidity position over the five year period should be seen as a cause for concern. This picture, as exhibited by the four key ratios selected, is not untypical for companies of this nature [1].

If the three main working capital elements (stock, work in progress

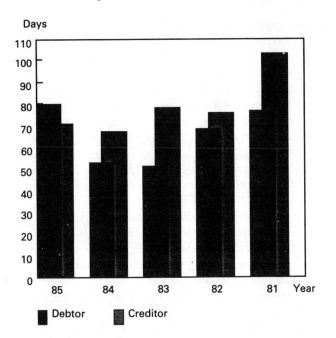

Figure 11.6 Debtor/creditor days

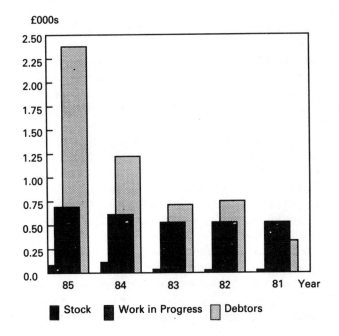

Figure 11.7 Stock/work-in-progress and debtors

and debtors – Figure 11.7) are considered in the light of high increases in turnover, then an interesting picture emerges. While stock and work-in-progress have behaved consistently, indicating good materials turnover and broadly similar 'work to be valued' levels over the five years, the debtor level element has increased drastically (slight fall in 1983). This has placed a heavier burden on company finances which in turn has resulted in an increased reliance on overdraft facilities.

In line with turnover increases the creditor level has also increased (Figure 11.6). However, in terms of the average number of days that monies were owed to creditors, a reasonably consistent pattern is exhibited. There were slight improvements in the payments picture in 1981/82.

If cashflow, as measured by the average debtor and creditor positions, is considered (Figure 11.6), it can be seen that both levels are rather high, with creditors being paid at a slightly faster rate than the receipt of monies from debtors in 1985. In all the previous years the reverse was true, payment to creditors being slower than money receipts.

Examination of the case study company's financial performance identifies a complicated picture where creditor/debtor levels are concerned. There is a tendency for a majority of clients to pay their debts early or at least on time, which helps to offset the effects of the minority of delinquent debtors. The same can be said for creditors, whereby the majority of suppliers/sub-contractors are paid reasonably quickly with only a minority of creditors having to wait for money.

The important factor to be considered for a company of this type will be its ability to monitor debtor/creditor levels and to comprehend the possible consequences of detrimental movements in cashflow. The management ratios set out in Figure 11.10 and discussed in the next section (Development of a corporate budget) attempt to set targets which seek gradually to improve the cashflow position.

The company's ability to meet its current liabilities, as measured by the current ratio and more critically by the acid test of cash-to-current liabilities (Figure 11.5), has remained consistent over the five years under consideration. That is to say, if a call was made for payment of monies to a major creditor or group of creditors, the company would have difficulty in meeting this without either increasing borrowing capacity or selling some assets. Many small to medium sized companies face similar problems to the case study company, and companies who are able to recognise a cashflow problem at an early stage are at least able to attempt appropriate measures to alleviate the situation.

It is worth drawing the above analysis to an end with some conclusions.

The company's financial performance can be summed up as follows. Turnover increases appear to have been adequately funded by the use of three approaches:

(1) Increases in share capital.
(2) Re-investment of profits.
(3) Controlled use of borrowed funds, both in the short term by an overdraft and in the long term through a loan arrangement.

The company operates in very competitive markets, only winning 1 in 7 contracts priced in competition, and the overall margins on turnover are very slim over the five years investigated. The figures mask what might be considered a complex situation. The company's margins on its speculative operations may well be quite high, while margins on competitively priced work could be very low. The overall effect produces a situation whereby the company's 'total costs' are only slightly exceeded by the 'total value' of the work being carried out. Thus, a 'book profit' could quite easily become a 'book loss' with such tight 'margins for error'.

Profitability has been on the increase, and this has been mainly due to a reasonable level of total capital 'turnover' and quite high shareholders' capital turnover rates. This can be illustrated as follows:

Company data for 1985 (Figure 11.3)	– Total capital turnover rate	= 6.18 times
	– Shareholders' capital turnover rate	= 12.16 times
Research findings based on 20 companies studied with 1984 accounts as a basis (Canter [1])	– Total capital turnover rate	= 6.01 times
	– Shareholder's capital turnover rate	= 5.73 times
Industry average in 1970 (Reynolds and Hesketh [40])	– Total capital turnover rate	= 3.6 times

Robertson [41] identified that a 2½% margin on turnover would produce a 20% return on capital employed, if capital employed is 'turned over' eight times in a year. In the case study company example, a 2.9% margin on turnover in 1985 produced:

ROCE (shareholders)   = 36.12% (SCTR = 12.16T)
ROCE (total)   = 18.35% (TCR = 6.18%)

It must be pointed out, however, that slow payments, for whatever reason, have a detrimental effect on capital turnover rates and subsequently on returns on capital employed.

Undermining the healthy overall 'book' picture is the poor cashflow status exhibited at the end of a trading period. Allied to this is the fact that problems could easily occur if a sudden call for monies was made by creditors. It must be noted however that the position shown in a company's audited accounts is based on figures collected at the end of a trading period. A company's performance may well vary considerably during a trading year. It is therefore important for any company to be able to set financial performance targets, using trend data generated from its accounts over several years. These performance targets can be used to monitor variances away from desired levels, on a regular basis through a trading year.

What follows is a demonstration of the approach to and nature of the data which can be produced using a company's existing published accounts. Such analysis can then be used to aid the production of a corporate budget and a set of performance ratios for a future trading period.

Development of a corporate budget

The corporate budget is the starting point for setting up a monitoring and reporting system. It also becomes the reference point at the end of a financial year, against which the measurement of financial performance and the achievement of planned objectives are made. The production of this budget will be a rolling exercise, looking back at past performance and taking advice from staff. For example, the managing director responsible for producing the budget will take advice from the estimator and other key personnel who will provide departmental market information.

Sufficient time should be allowed for the research and advice-taking procedures, in order that a firm budget can be finalised by the board of directors prior to the beginning of the trading period concerned. It is suggested that an outline master budget is produced at least six months prior to the commencement of a trading period, which should then give adequate time to apply any necessary changes to suit movements in market conditions.

Establishment of a return on capital employed target

When considering the measurement of financial performance, the starting point will normally be the return achieved on the capital employed in the business. This is usually put forward as the key performance measurement ratio when considering a company's efficiency-of-use of its total assets [41]. Many writers when considering a structured approach to the use of financial ratios within a perform-ance measurement system talk in terms of a ROCE pyramid [37,38] whereby the ROCE ratio is the most important and is depicted at the apex of a pyramid.

If each contract undertaken is considered in the same light as any other investment which the company can enter into, then it is reason-able for the company to set a target for ROCE in the light of investment opportunities.

Therefore, the required rate of return will be the absolute lowest yield that a company can accept while still maintaining its commitment to a set of objectives for a given period. A company's mark-up on costs, over all contracts, should at the very least achieve this 'required re-turn'. However, companies cannot just state a 'required rate of return' and then set out to achieve this over a period of time. Any required rate of return will be influenced by a number of factors and thus must be set at an achievable level.

Factors which should be taken into account when setting the re-quired ROCE target are:

(1) Company needs and objectives over a trading period.
(2) Competition in the market place and its effect on profit margins.
(3) The cost of finance to achieve the desired turnover.

The sources of finance needed to carry out contracts can be divided into two distinct classifications:

(a) External sources costing a market interest rate measured by the risks perceived by the lenders.
(b) Internal sources, generated from the company's operations and costing an interest level, by virtue of the money being 'locked up' in a contract for a period of time and thus losing its interest-bearing capacity (the interest level could also be considered as 'opportunity cost').

Consider a company which has no working capital generated from operations and therefore has to use borrowed funds at anything from 18% to 21% interest p.a. If in a very competitive market this company is having to tender for work 'at cost' (profit = zero) then the required rate of return would of necessity be the interest rate charged (18–21%) in order for this company to maintain its repayments.

Therefore any company must commence calculating its ROCE target from the level at which it requires to maintain its repayment liabilities, and from this level percentages can be added for profit and risk until a required ROCE target is arrived at which is in line with company objectives.

This marginal costing approach can be very useful not only as a target setting medium, in the short term, but can also be incorporated into a monitoring and control system, which is vital in the case of highly geared companies if they are to maintain their short-term commitments.

Example: Build-up of a required ROCE target (using the case study company data with year ending December 1989 as the forecasting period)

It is assumed that the board of directors is seeking an increase in turnover to a level of £2.2 million for the period in question. Also assumed is that the company will continue to rely on a mixture of borrowed funds and re-investment. The ROCE target can then be evaluated as follows:

(1) The average weighted cost of capital	8%
(2) Profit margin to generate a level of turnover and from this a return on company resources invested in contracts at an acceptable level	3%
(3) A contingency to cover uncertainties (risk factor)	1%
(4) Miscellaneous corporate obligations such as dividends, additions to capital reserves, taxation and depreciation allowances	8%
Required ROCE (total capital employed) (before tax)	20%

It is very important that this calculation is constantly monitored and adjusted to reflect the company's competitiveness in the market place. If the company is running an effective cost/value reconciliation system [25] on its contracts, this will enable the contribution each contract is making towards both overheads and the ROCE target to be assessed regularly and, if necessary, adjustments made.

The ROCE target calculated above has been included in Figure 11.10, and this constitutes one of the management ratios against which actual performance will be measured.

If small to medium sized companies of comparable turnover, operating in a discrete market, are considered, then there is a high likelihood that the direct costs of building will be the same for each company. If this is the case then a company's effectiveness will be based largely on its ability to control the components which make up the ROCE target as well as company overheads. This does assume, however, that a reasonably efficient cost control system is also in operation.

The ROCE target and its achievement are influenced by the company's expectations for income and growth, and management's stategic plan to meet expectations.

The return on capital consists of a series of contributions generated by a programme of contracts.

Each contract uses varying amounts of the company's working capital, which is finite, over different periods of time.

A company will need to consider the following objectives when assessing the contributions that each contract will or can make towards achieving an overall ROCE target:

(1) To ensure that the sum of the contributions from all its contracts meet the overall ROCE target.
(2) To assess the contributions which, other things being equal, a particular contract should make.
(3) To determine the pattern of demands on working capital, how much and for how long, both for specific contracts and for the company's contract programme as a whole. This will establish the company cashflow pattern. This pattern will indicate whether working capital is:
(a) Under-used – more work could be envisaged.
(b) Inadequate – more finance is needed.

Working capital is every bit as much a resource as skilled labour, materials and management ability. A lack of working capital and an incomplete understanding of the need to plan its use are primary reasons for a high proportion of the enforced and voluntary liquidations encountered in the industry.

Assessment of working capital requirements

In trying to assess how much working capital a company will require at any given turnover level, the only realistic approach is to produce detailed cashflow forecasts for each contract undertaken.

When attempting to estimate the amount of working capital for a future period, detailed cashflow calculations for previous contracts may or may not be available. Jones [42], supported by Reynolds and Hesketh [40], showed that under United Kingdom contractual conditions a builder needs to set aside one-eighth of annual turnover as working capital actually employed on contracts. The total capital required may well be much more if offices and land are being purchased, or if plant or large stocks of materials are being held. If a controlled approach is adopted, whereby land is purchased using a mortgage, plant is hired and stock is efficiently employed, a 1:5 working capital to turnover ratio might be more realistic.

Having established a level of working capital to suit the particular turnover desired, the next step is to develop the relationships between return on capital employed, return on equity capital and profit on turnover so that a forecast balance sheet, a profit statement and management ratios can be established.

Key relationships within the system

It was established earlier that the case study company has a desired turnover level of £2.2 million for the coming trading period. A return on total capital employed (before tax) was also set earlier at 20%. In order to achieve this desired turnover level a 3% profit on turnover percentage has been selected as the most suitable, considering the competitiveness of the markets in which it operates. Therefore:

Profit on turnover = £2 200 000 × 3/100 = £66 000

Hence, using the required return on total capital of 20%:

Total capital employed = £330 000 (found from £66 000 = TCE/5)

of which in this case: £32 080 is share capital
£11 766 is preference shares/debentures
£132 920 is capital reserves
£153 234 is loans

Using these figures the forecast balance sheet (Figure 11.8), profit statement (Figure 11.9) and management ratios (Figure 11.10) can be developed.

Return on equity capital is seen to be £66 000/£165 000 = 40%

and

Capital turnover rate = £2 200 000/300 000 = 6.6 times

It can also be demonstrated that the return on total capital employed is the direct product of profit on turnover, on the one hand, and the rate of capital turned over, on the other. This is shown as:

3% × 6.66t = 19.98 or approx. 20%

The relationships discussed above enable the forecast statements to be produced. However, it must be pointed out that capital turnover rates can vary widely, depending on trading conditions and the risks taken by companies. Depending on capital structure (gearing), trading policy and attitude to risk, equity capital might represent one-tenth (high gearing) or nine-tenths (low gearing) of the total capital employed.

It does not matter how many times capital is turned over or whether a company is highly or lowly geared, the relationships identified earlier still apply.

One concept that should be highligted is that of 'leverage' [39]. Companies with sufficiently high gearing that are able to turn capital over at high rates can enhance their shareholders' returns or re-investment opportunities even with very low profit margins.

It is important and clearly very useful for companies to be able to measure their own profit performance against other similar companies operating in common markets. Profit targets must be set in the light of what is achievable in a market and be at such a level that work is acquired in line with the turnover levels desired.

The forecast balance sheet, profit statement and management ratios

The procedures presented and discussed in the preceding sections will now be used to produce a forecast balance sheet.

Figure 11.8 depicts this statement, which requires some explanation and comment. Fixed assets are valued at either cost less depreciation or an assessment of market value. An allowance is also made for additions or sales in line with company objectives. Working capital has been allowed for at one-quarter of turnover, in line with the comments made earlier in this chapter. The debtor level reflects a target for the average number of days the company will be owed money over a trading period, and has been set at 56 days. Figure 11.10 identifies the debtor days' positions and also shows that 60 is the average number of days for which the company will owe money. These two targets ident-ify the need to receive money before payments are made and also take account of contractual arrangements.

The capital employed figure was established earlier. At this level, there is a need to increase the company's borrowing commitment from £74 038 (level at present) to £153 324 (107% increase). Reserves are also

Balance sheet for the year ending December 1989

	£	£
Fixed assets (net)	230 000	230 000
Current assets		
Stock	30 136	
Work in progress	179 075	
Debtors	337 534	
Cash at bank and on deposit	3 255	
Total assets	780 000	
Current liabilities		
Creditors	360 000	
Overdraft	50 000	
Taxation	40 000	
Dividend	—	
Net current assets		100 000
Capital employed		330 000
Financed by:		
Share capital		32 080
Reserves		132 920
Loans		153 234
Preference shares/Debentures		11 766
Funds employed		330 000

Figure 11.8   Forecasted balance sheet

required to increase from £56 497 (level at present) to £132 920 (135%).
This requires emphasis on a re-investment policy which, in terms of
the cost of finance, needs to be measured against both 'opportunity
costs' and the cost of finance in the market place.

Figure 11.9 shows the forecast profit statement. The turnover figure
is the desired level set by the board of directors.

If the same types and mix of work are continued, then production
costs and administrative expenses are highly likely to remain a consistent proportion of turnover. Both these 'costs' have been included in
Figure 11.9 using the trend analysis presented earlier. The net profit
before tax and interest figure represents a 3% margin on turnover. A
1% risk factor has been levied for unforeseen circumstances. Interest
and preference dividend payments are in line with contract conditions
agreed with the providers of funds.

Taxation will be levied at the current rate of corporation tax, after
suitable allowances have been made against profits [43].

Profit statement for the year ending December 1989

	£
Turnover	2 200 000
Production costs	1 892 000
Administration expenses	220 000
Performance variance (risk factor) 1%	22 000
Net profit before tax and interest	66 000
Interest paid/Preference dividend	42 900
Taxation	4 500
Net profit after tax and interest	18 600

Figure 11.9   Forecasted profit statement

Figure 11.10 sets out the forecast management ratios which have been calculated in line with the forecast performance levels discussed and presented in Figures 11.8 and 11.9.

The next step is to produce the corporate budget which uses the data forecast in the balance sheet, profit statement and management ratios, and will become the central statement in the management accounting framework of the control system. It is also the key statement used at level 1 in the responsibility reporting system (see Figure 11.11).

The corporate budget – the benchmark for performance measurement

Using the information produced in the previous sections, a master or corporate budget has been produced for the case study company. This constitutes an agreed statement of a set of desired outcomes which can be used to monitor progress.

Figure 11.12 depicts the master budget against which reports from lower levels can be compared (see chapter 7).

As can be seen, the anticipated turnover for the twelve month period is £2 200 000. This is made up of work, 59% of which has been secured and 41% is to be secured. The managing director will now be in a position, at least 6 months prior to the beginning of the trading period, to decide on a strategy to secure the proportion of turnover required.

The managing director will need to discuss with the company's estimator the possibility of obtaining a sufficient number of enquiries. These then must be processed to give a reasonable lead time in order to achieve start dates which generate the required turnover. This

Management ratios for year ending December 1989	
Overall Performance	
ROCE (Shareholders)	40%
ROCE (Total)	20%
PBTI/Turnover	3
Turnover/Shareholders' Funds	13.3T
Turnover/Funds Employed	6.67T
Solvency	
Capital owned/Capital employed	50%
PBTI/Fixed Interest Payments	1.53T
Liquidity	
Current ratio	1.22
Acid test	0.76
Debtor days	56 days
Creditor days	60 days
CAFA	2.39
Market Tests	
Return on Equity	11%
Earnings/Share	56p

Figure 11.10   Forecasted management ratios

procedure also gives the estimator an opportunity to consider the cost of operating this function as part of the budgeting process.

In 1987 this company's tender success rate was one in seven contracts. It must be appreciated that the cost of producing six unsuccessful tenders out of every seven can only be recovered on contracts which are secured. All building companies who operate in competitive markets are faced with this dilemma.

Clearly they face two choices, either attempt to reduce estimating costs by being more selective in tendering (only tendering where there is a high chance of success [2]), or budget for these costs and rely on the contracts actually carried out making sufficient contributions to company overheads to sustain a highly inefficient approach to acquiring work [44]. The first approach, that of being more selective, is considered the most sensible of the two options. This, of course, must depend a great deal on market conditions.

It is clear that in order to achieve the £2.2 million desired turnover, the company must tender for and acquire £900 000 of work of various types. In setting these targets, account must be taken of the level of

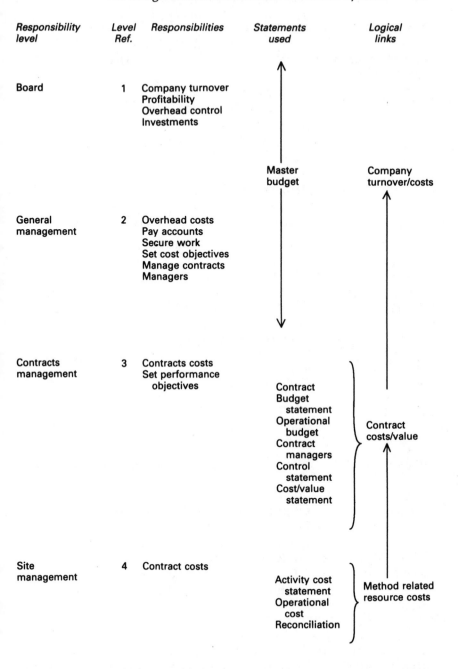

Responsibility level	Level Ref.	Responsibilities	Statements used	Logical links
Board	1	Company turnover Profitability Overhead control Investments		
			Master budget	Company turnover/costs
General management	2	Overhead costs Pay accounts Secure work Set cost objectives Manage contracts Managers		
Contracts management	3	Contracts costs Set performance objectives	Contract Budget statement Operational budget Contract managers Control statement Cost/value statement	Contract costs/value
Site management	4	Contract costs	Activity cost statement Operational cost Reconciliation	Method related resource costs

Figure 11.11 Responsibility reporting system

Responsibilities	*Outline budget for 12 months ending*	*Period*
Company turnover Profitability		December 1989
Overhead control	Turnover in hand now	1 300 000
Investments	Work to be obtained	900 000
	Anticipated turnover	2 200 000
	Average margins at tender stage (overheads and profit)	330 000
	Performance variation	(22 000)
	Total contribution from contracts (1)	308 000
	Overhead costs & interest:	
	Estimating function	20 000
	Surveying function	20 000
	Production function	60 000
	Buying function	20 000
	Administration function	80 000
	Interest on working capital	20 000
	Total overheads & interest (2)	220 000
	Net contribution ((1)−(2))	88 000
	SSAP9 Provision 1	(10 000)
	SSAP9 Provision 2	(5 000)
	Net profit	73 000

Control targets		
Contribution %age	14%	Gross (of Turnover)
Contribution %age	4%	Net (of Turnover)
Overhead %age	10%	(of Turnover)
Production costs %age	86%	(of Turnover)
Net profit %age	3%	(of Turnover)

Figure 11.12   Pro-forma for master budget

competitiveness within the markets operated. The company must then decide in which areas it could be most successful in winning work, and operate a pricing policy which is likely to produce successful tenders.

The next step is to consider the contribution that must be forthcoming from the contract work if the £2.2 million turnover is to be achieved. This contribution forms part of a contract manager's responsibility and represents an important indicator that needs to be identified in the control reports produced. Chapter 7 discusses the concept of responsibility levels and cost reporting.

In this case the company is looking for an average of 15% across the board at the tender stage. It is one thing to set a margin at the tender stage, but quite another to achieve it in the final account.

The variation which could occur in this average tender margin next needs to be assessed, using contract report information. The adjusted contract contribution will then form another key assessment target to be monitored from the control reports.

The managing director is responsible for the costs of the various functions required to be performed in the running of the business, and another key assessment target will be the £220 000 in respect of overheads and interest charges (Figure 11.12).

The net contribution of £88 000 (4% margin on turnover) constitutes a target profit margin which, once adjusted by the various performance variances, can be compared with the margin eventually published in the financial accounts. The reference point here is the value of £66 000 net profit before tax and interest in the forecast profit statement (Figure 11.9).

The value of £88 000 needs to be adjusted not only in respect of performance variances, but also in line with the provisions of Statement of Standard Accounting Practice No. 9 [21]. The effect of S.S.A.P.9 for a construction company is twofold:

(1) It restricts the declaration of profits in the audited accounts and requires declaration on a different time scale from the one that contractors are accustomed to. This only affects the so-called long-term contracts of a small company – contracts which transcend trading periods.
(2) Contractors must make provision for future losses. These may occur by anticipating the payment of claims which do not materialise, or simply over-spending on contracts.

While these provisions apply to the way a company's financial statements are presented, it is also necessary for the requirements to be incorporated within the management accounts in order that a fair comparative medium is maintained. There is also a close link here with future cashflow considerations.

At the bottom of the pro-forma (Figure 11.12) are the control targets for comparison with data produced in the control reports from lower levels in the responsibility chain. Each of these control targets can be apportioned across the range of activities performed by the company.

This approach to producing initially a budget outline and subsequently the master budget enables the managing director to set initial targets for each of the functional areas responsible to him – covering establishment criteria and capital expenditure as well as principal operational responsibilities, even if these are his own responsibility. The time gap between the production of the outline budget and a final master budget allows for the setting of attainable targets in the light of company circumstances. Figure 11.13 illustrates this process.

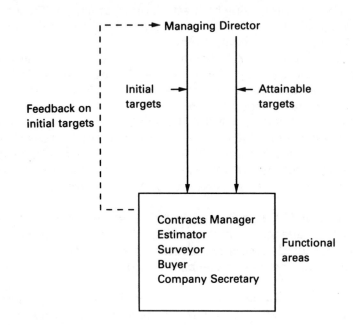

Figure 11.13   Budgeting process

Contract contribution and its relationship to ROCE

A return on capital employed target was established earlier in this chapter. This target did not include an element for general overheads, to which all the company's contracts are required to contribute. The following example demonstrates how a contribution is earned from the use of a finite amount of working capital.

Example: Forecast for year ending December 1989

Total capital employed   = £330 000
Net current assets   = £100 000 (net working capital)

ROCE target   = 20%
General overheads   = £220 000 (including interest)
Therefore 20% of £330 000   = £ 66 000
Plus overheads   = £220 000
Required total contribution   = £286 000 from contracts

This contribution of £286 000 has to be earned from the use of £100 000 of net or free working capital (see Figure 11.8). Therefore the average return required on contract investment is:

$$\frac{286\ 000}{100\ 000} \times \frac{100}{1} = 286\%$$

This apparently high return on contract investment is due to a heavy commitment to borrowing and reliance on the use of creditors, and is based on the investment of money into one or several contracts.

The percentage margin required on direct costs of construction (estimated cost) is calculated as follows:

Desired company turnover = £2 200 000
Less   = £ 286 000 (total contribution)
Gross cost of construction = £1 914 000

Therefore the gross margin required to be added to 'cost' for overheads and profit is:

$$\frac{286\ 000}{1\ 914\ 000} \times \frac{100}{1} = 15\%$$

Management needs to add 15% to the estimated costs in order to turn an estimate into a tender, in order that overheads and profit are covered.

If the case study company carries out ten contracts all of the same size, then:

$$\frac{1\ 914\ 000}{10} = £191\ 400\ \text{average construction cost or direct cost of construction per contract}$$

Therefore

$$£1\ 914\ 000 \times \frac{15}{100} = £28\ 710\ \text{contribution required from each contract towards overheads and profit}$$

As a check, 10 × £287 100 is the period contribution, which represents a £1100 over-recovery on the series of ten contracts or £110 per contract. This is explained by the rounding-up of the gross margin percentage, and acts as an extra contingency factor.

This relationship between return on capital employed and return on contract investment (net working capital), together with the margins required on costs to achieve both, become central components of the company's cost/value reconciliation system, which in turn is the central element of the company's financial monitoring and control procedures.

Time value of working capital

In chapter 10 the effects of delayed payment on the ultimate return on capital employed on a contract were considered. Up to the point at which a contract becomes self-financing a certain level of money will be 'locked up' in the contract and cannot be used in other aspects of the business. Some of this money has been borrowed by the company to finance the work and thus will incur an interest charge as payment for its use. A proportion of money on any contract will be owed to creditors, and the discounts allowed for prompt payment should be compared with the 'cost of borrowed funds', because the use of creditors' entitlements is a recognised method of alleviating cashflow pressure in the short term [42]. Up until the client pays for part or all of the work carried out, the money owing can be considered to be losing interest, because the contractor cannot use this money for business activities.

For a company this represents a rather complex situation with many inflows and outflows of funds requiring constant adjustment of working capital levels. If a contract proceeds faster than expected or a client suddenly becomes slow in paying, extra funds may well be required.

A company therefore needs to be able to measure the cost effects of using differing amounts of working capital, and this can be represented as an interest charge.

Cooke and Jepson [26] and Harris and McCaffer [28] all examine methods of producing a compound measure of the time and usage of working capital. This compound measure of capital used over a time period is identified as CAPTIM (Capital × Time). Their approaches have been employed to substantiate the contribution assessments made and to establish an interest charge for the working capital deployed on a contract or series of contracts.

Example: CAPTIM assessment

£100 000 has been identified as the amount of free capital available for the 12-month trading period. If the time effect is brought to bear, a compound measure of '£ × months' can be produced:

Working capital × Time = CAPTIM = £100 000 × 12

$$= 1\ 200\ 000\ £\ months$$

This concept can be represented as follows:

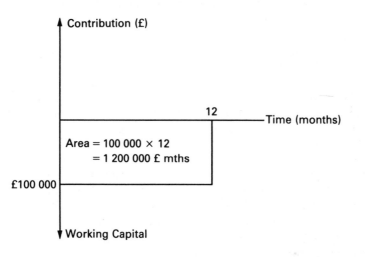

If one contract is considered and this runs for 6 months and draws £50 000 of working capital which fluctuates from 0 to £50 000 to 0, then this can be represented as:

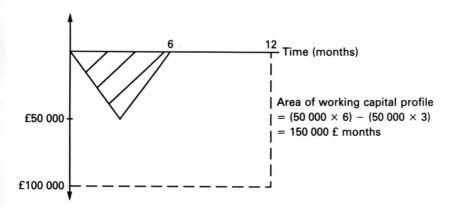

Thus from the total working capital fund (£100 000) with a required total contribution of £286 000, the *pro-rata* contribution for this one contract, return on capital invested over a 6-month period, is calculated as:

$$\frac{150\ 000}{1\ 200\ 000} \times £286\ 000 = £35\ 750$$

This approach to contribution assessment, based on working capital usage, should be used with great care. Many other considerations will need to be taken into account, such as:

(1) The calculation assumes 100% effective use of working capital throughout the year, but this is highly unlikely.
(2) The company's reasons for seeking a particular contract may not be a rate of return. Such factors as maintaining market share, prestigious work and lack of the desired turnover might be considered more important in the short term.

The importance of this approach lies in its ease of use as part of the budgeting process and subsequently as a means of monitoring and controlling the effects of contractual decisions taken. For example, if a contract is entered into, for reasons other than a contribution being made, the financial implications can be identified and the effects on the company's other operations and in particular the effect on overall company cashflow can be evaluated.

The CAPTIM measure can also be used to calculate the cost (interest charge) of the working capital deployed on a contract or series of contracts. If the company uses an overdraft facility to support its short-term finance needs then the interest charge for this contract is identified as:

$$\text{Interest charge} = \frac{\text{CAPTIM}}{12\ (\text{months})} \times \frac{\text{Rate}}{100}$$

In this case the interest or opportunity cost is 20%. Therefore for the contract the interest is:

$$\frac{150\ 000}{12} \times \frac{20}{100} = £2500$$

and for the series of contracts over 12 months:

$$\frac{1\ 120\ 000}{12} \times \frac{20}{100} = £20\ 000$$

The above interest charge has been used in the master budget (see Figure 11.12).

This enables a level of interest to be allowed within contract contributions and becomes a reference point for the comparison of actual interest charged on short-term borrowings over the trading period.

A system of control levels

Chapter 7 identified the notion of control by means of responsibility levels which can be established in a company. Also identified was the problem of differentiation, whereby it is difficult to separate levels of operation or responsibilities within smaller organisations. The importance of being able to collect cost data in describable and manageable units is perhaps the important criterion within a control system, and this idea is developed here within the responsibility framework.

Control responsibilities

Figure 11.14 illustrates the structuring of cost data under control responsibility levels for the case study company.

As can be seen, each cost element is broken down into its component parts which can then form the basis of a control report produced by the person allocated responsibility for a control level. It is considered desirable to produce these control reports on standard forms and that the data used at each reporting level are clearly referenced to data used at other levels. This is seen as not only an *aide-memoire* to report producers, but also an important criterion for integration and control of data usage.

Monitoring and control at contracts management level

The next step in the model system is the monitoring and reporting procedures at contracts management level. It is at this level that the monitoring of actual cashflow on a contract and its comparison with estimated cashflow take place.

The contracts manager(s) have to produce a budget statement, with the help of a surveyor, if one is employed, for each project under their control. This statement will be based on the estimates produced to obtain the work. The main problem here is one of detail. Companies make tender offers under a variety of conditions, ranging from offers

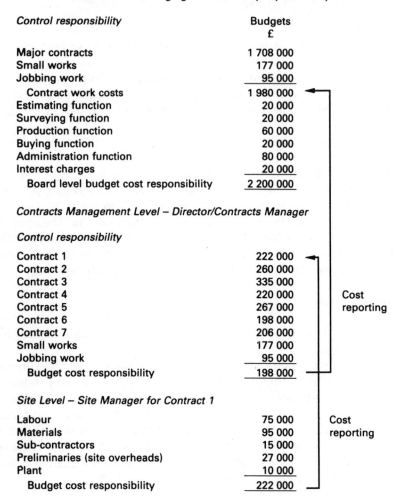

Board Level – Managing Director/Company Secretary

Control responsibility	Budgets £
Major contracts	1 708 000
Small works	177 000
Jobbing work	95 000
Contract work costs	1 980 000
Estimating function	20 000
Surveying function	20 000
Production function	60 000
Buying function	20 000
Administration function	80 000
Interest charges	20 000
Board level budget cost responsibility	2 200 000

Contracts Management Level – Director/Contracts Manager

Control responsibility

Contract 1	222 000	
Contract 2	260 000	
Contract 3	335 000	
Contract 4	220 000	Cost
Contract 5	267 000	reporting
Contract 6	198 000	
Contract 7	206 000	
Small works	177 000	
Jobbing work	95 000	
Budget cost responsibility	198 000	

Site Level – Site Manager for Contract 1

Labour	75 000	Cost
Materials	95 000	reporting
Sub-contractors	15 000	
Preliminaries (site overheads)	27 000	
Plant	10 000	
Budget cost responsibility	222 000	

Figure 11.14 Cost responsibility levels

calculated using bills of quantities, involving a high level of price/cost breakdown, to lump sum jobbing work quotations calculated on a time and materials basis. A decision therefore has to be made which establishes the nature of cost breakdown under a variety of pricing approaches and which facilitates monitoring and control.

No matter what approach is adopted to pricing, each contract can be broken down into a set of repetitive cost units which in turn can be broken down into individual resources.

Job 1   Contract Budget Statement   Date: 15 February 1989
(amounts in £s)

Operations (cost units)	Labour	Materials	Plant	Sub-Contractors	Cost total	Value	Margin
Preliminaries (including staff)	21 450	6 300	14 750	1 000	43 500	36 225	4 725
Substructure	7 500	12 500	5 000	—	25 000	28 750	3 750
Frame	9 000	12 000	—	9 000	30 000	34 500	4 500
Exterior walls	4 500	7 500	—	3 000	15 000	17 250	2 250
Interior walls	3 000	7 000	—	—	10 000	11 500	1 500
Roof	4 000	6 000	—	—	10 000	11 500	1 500
Services	3 000	5 500	—	—	8 500	9 775	1 275
First fix (woodwork)	—	—	—	30 000	30 000	34 500	4 500
Finishes	4 000	5 000	—	—	9 000	10 350	1 350
Second fix (woodwork)	—	—	—	20 000	20 000	23 000	3 000
Decorations	—	—	—	10 000	10 000	11 500	1 500
External works	—	—	—	7 000	7 000	8 050	1 050
Snagging	2 000	1 000	—	—	3 000	3 450	450
Final clean	—	—	—	1 000	1 000	1 150	150
Cost/Value Totals	58 450	62 800	19 750	81 000	222 000	241 500	31 500

Figure 11.15 Contract budget statement pro-forma

The contract budget

Figure 11.15 illustrates the above approach using information for con-tract 1 shown in Figure 11.14.

The data shown in Figure 11.15 come from the tender breakdown for the contract. The cost units selected are those that normally occur on the majority of contracts, and the approach illustrated should lead to the design of a company pro-forma.

Note the introduction of a value column which enables the margin between cost and value to be monitored.

Having produced a budget statement for each contract, the next stage will be to consider;

(1) The type and detail required of reports to go to board level.
(2) Monitoring and controlling costs against budgets.

If (2) is considered in the first instance, then cost/value information in the contract budget statement (Figure 11.15) must be spread across the contract programme so that cost and value are set in their relevant time zones. From this, the production of expenditure and revenue budgets is facilitated by identifying the actual income and expenditure dates.

The operational budget

Figure 11.16 illustrates the type of summary which should be produced using a contract programme. This enables the contracts manager to monitor operation costs on a monthly basis.

It is worth noting that the statements produced at each level have two primary functions:

(1) To provide managers with cost data on a need-to-know basis – information in statements should be summarised to suit monitoring needs. Each statement would normally be produced using data which have been analysed in much more detail.
(2) To enable managers at each level to take decisions or implement corrective action when necessary.

The contracts manager, using the details shown in Figure 11.16, can now produce, on a monthly basis, a control statement for himself and also a contract manager's report.

The control statement

Figure 11.17 identifies the form that the control statement might take, and as can be seen a month-by-month comparison of costs can be achieved.

The pro-forma statements shown in Figures 11.17 and 11.18 are for the contract manager's own use. Depending on the detail required, he or the quantity surveyor will have produced these using a considerable amount of back-up information. The next step is to produce a report to go to board level which conveys the current cost and value status of a contract. If the company does employ a surveyor, then this task will be carried out by him after analysing the valuation position. Having said this, the contracts manager is still responsible for the overall monitoring and control of cost and value on his contracts; the surveyor's function is to provide timely cost and value data for inclusion in the reporting system.

Valuation statement of cash inflow

It is of vital importance that the value of the work carried out is accurately monitored and adequately recorded and presented for agreement and subsequent payment by the client.

Job Nr 1 *Operational Budget*
(amounts in £s)

Date: 15 February 1989
Contract duration: 12 months

Operations	Month: Budget cost total	March Budget cost	March Budget value	March Budget margin	April Budget cost	April Budget value	April Budget margin	May Budget cost	May Budget value	May Budget margin
[Prelims]	31 500	4 500	5 175	675	3 000	3 450	450	3 000	3 450	450
[Site staff]	12 000	1 000	1 150	150	1 000	1 150	150	1 000	1 150	150
Substruct.	25 000	10 000	11 500	1 500	10 000	10 000	1 500	5 000	5 750	750
Frame	30 000	—	—	—	—	—	—	2 000	2 300	300
Ext. walls	15 000	—	—	—	—	—	—	1 000	1 150	150
Int. walls	10 000									
Roof	10 000									
Services	8 500							1 000	1 150	150
1st fix (woodwork)	30 000									
Finishes	9 000									
2nd fix (woodwork)	20 000									
Decorations	10 000									
Ext. works	7 000									
Snagging	3 000									
Final clean	1 000									
	210 000									
Monthly totals		15 500	17 825	2 325	14 000	16 100	2 100	13 000	14 950	1 950
Cumulative totals		15 500	17 825	2 325	29 500	33 925	4 425	42 500	48 875	6 375

Notes:
1. Monthly totals enable the monthly cost target to be monitored.
2. Cumulative totals enable the total period cost to be viewed.

Figure 11.16 Contracts manager's operational budget (only three months of a 12-month budget shown)

Project Nr 1   *Contract Manager's Control Statement* Period: 3
                       (amounts in £s)

Item	May 1989 Actual	Estimated	Variance	Previous month (April) Actual	Estimated	Variance
Materials delivered	38 250			18 950		
Less on site & not fixed	20 000			5 000		
Materials fixed	18 250	16 250	(2 000)	13 950	13 750	(200)
Labour	14 000	13 000	(1 000)	8 350	8 250	(100)
Plant	6 250	6 250	—	2 600	2 600	—
Own direct work	38 500	35 500	(3 000)	24 900	24 600	(300)
Sub-contractors	4 500	4 000	(500)	1 000	900	(100)
Preliminaries (staff costs)	3 000	3 000	—	2 000	2 000	—
Contract cost totals	46 000	42 500	(3 500)	27 900	27 500	(400)

Figure 11.17   Control statement pro-forma

There are a number of reasons why a contract might be under- or
over-valued. Disagreements as to how much work has been carried
out, the value of variations to the work as originally envisaged and of
course negligence might all play a part. A contractor might deliberately
over- or under-value the work for particular cashflow purposes. It is
important for the contractor to be aware that the amount of retention
held, if a standard form of contract is employed, will be based on the
interim valuation of the work. Retention monies are 'locked up' on the
contract until release points are reached, and it is clearly very important that a reasonable level of retention is held, releases of retention are
correctly facilitated and a final account is agreed as soon after contract
completion as possible [45].

Variations, agreement and payment

From the day that a project is contemplated to the day that the client
can make use of the completed building, the type and nature of the
building can vary considerably.

The contractor is required to produce a forecast of cost based on
drawings and contract documentation provided at the tender stage.
Having been chosen to carry out the work, there might well be a high

probability that the work, as costed at tender stage, will change or necessarily be varied, as in the case of maintenance or refurbishment, where unforeseen defects are encountered. It is also difficult to assess the amount of change requested by a client or his representatives. The majority of the standard forms of contract [31, 32] incorporate variation clauses which provide a mechanism for valuing variations as and when they occur. These clauses are very similar in the wording of the definition of what might constitute a variation, and the following is a reasonable interpretation of a typical variation clause:

'alteration or modification of the design, quality or quantity of the work including the addition, omission or substitution of any work.'

All the standard clauses identify restrictions to change in the nature of the work, nevertheless variations on occasions can be major and have serious cost consequences.

If a standard form of contract is used, then a set of rules for identifying and valuing variations exists. If one is not used then a set of guidelines must be agreed between the contractor and the client at an early stage.

Variations might occur for the following reasons:

(1) The client/architect decide to change the original design to save money.
(2) The design was not clearly conceived at the outset, and changes or adaptations are required to produce a workable finished building.
(3) An unforeseen circumstance occurs, which requires a change to facilitate the work being efficiently carried out.

Once a variation has occurred it is important that it is first identified. Agreement that it has caused a change in the nature of the work must be sought, and from this a valuation must be made to ensure that payment ensues in order that cashflow on a contract is adequately maintained.

An instruction to vary the work must be issued in some form, or a decision to make a change must be taken by someone in the contractor's organisation.

The following control procedures are put forward as being the minimum necessary for the management of variations on projects:

(1) The change in the nature of the work must be clearly identified with the scope and consequences of the change being agreed by all parties as early as possible.
(2) The variation must be adequately measured and valued, at best

before the work is actually carried out, and a record kept of the amounts to be agreed. Figure 11.18 is a suggested format for use within the model system.

(3) As soon as the work is carried out, a request for payment, including a valuation or invoice, should be made promptly. A record of agreed amounts, and amounts outstanding, with any reasons for disagreements, should be maintained.

A procedure such as the above should form an integral part of the contractor's control system for each contract, and should clearly identify cashflow implications for the company as a whole [45].

Utilising a form like that shown in Figure 11.18, the financial position of variations on a contract can be seen at a glance. The 'Amount Outstanding' and 'Expected Final Amount' columns indicate future cash inflows and, together with the reasons for the outstanding amounts shown, enable management to instigate appropriate action as necessary.

Reconciliations

Figure 11.19 shows the type of report which can be produced using data from valuations and the control statements shown in Figures 11.18, 11.19 and 11.20.

The cost/value statement provides the managing director with not only the areas where questions should be asked, but also a prediction of the possible final account level and with this the contract cashflow status.

The results of the above exercise can be compared with the forecasts produced at tender stage.

These analyses not only constitute the monitoring and control medium but also enable the company's database of contract information to be enhanced and expanded for future use.

Monitoring and control at site level

The final control aspects to consider are control and reporting at site level.

At site level the concern is for comparison of resource costs, labour, materials and plant, included in the estimate for cost units, with those actually incurred and recorded on labour allocation sheets, materials invoices and plant returns.

The site manager is interested in the cost efficiency of each individual activity within a group of cost units, e.g. concrete in foundations aspect of the foundations grouping.

Project Nr 1

V.O. Nr Origin	Forecast of value (amounts in £s)			Current situation						
	Min.	Max.	Expected	Addition*	Saving*	Amount included in valuation	Date of valuation	Amount outstanding	Expected final amount	Reasons/Remarks
1	450	500	450	450		400	29/3/89 (1)	150	450	Not agreed
2	(1 000)	(1 700)	(1 500)		(1 500)	(1 400)	"		(1 500)	Work to be done
3	2 000	2 500	2 300	2 300		2 000	29/4/89 (2)	300	2 300	Work to be done
Arch's letter 6/3/89 Drg Nr 123 Rev. F	(1 000)	(1 000)	(1 000)		(1 000)	(1 000)	"		(1 000)	
4	500	700	600	600		500	29/5/89 (3)	100	600	Not agreed
5	3 000	3 000	3 000	3 000		3 000	"		3 000	
	5 000	5 000		5 000					5 000	Work to be done
	8 950	9 000		11 350	(2 500)	3 500		450	8 850	

* These two columns show additions or savings to the contract sum. This is important because revenue should not be anticipated and the nearer the true position, the better the cashflow forecast.

Figure 11.18 Variation control

Project Nr 1 (Amounts in £s)	Cost/Value Statement		Period: 3 Month: May Work in progress
	Current	*Project final value*	
Q.S. valuation & certificate	66 600	251 500	Current value 66 600
Under-/Over-valuation	5 000	—	Cash received 60 000
Adjusted internal value	61 600	251 500	Work in progress 6 600
Contract cost	56 000	232 500	Retention 3 330
			Over-valuation
Margin	5 600	19 000	value 5 000
Tender margin	7 875	31 500	
Margin variance	(2 275)	(12 500)	Value increment
Variance on estimated costs			since last
Materials	(2 000)	(6 000)	valuation 26 350
Labour	(1 000)	(3 000)	
Plant	—	—	
Own direct work	(3 000)	(9 000)	
Sub-contractors	(500)	(1 000)	
Preliminaries (staff costs)	—	—	
Cost variance total	(3 500)	(10 000)	
Variations to date			
Included in valuations	3 500		
Identified but not included	5 000	16 000	
Variations total	8 500	16 000	

Figure 11.19   Cost/value statement produced by contract manager/ surveyor

Basic approaches to cost monitoring

There are three basic approaches that can be adopted by a site manager when attempting to monitor cost on contracts:

(1) Monitor and produce a report for the contracts manager on every activity on site on a weekly/monthly basis. This requires the labour and plant allocation sheets and materials received sheets to be analysed in detail and then compared with the estimated activity costs in the tender. This is a very time-consuming exercise and might not prove very cost-effective in the long term, although it could form the basis of a comprehensive feedback system.

(2) Use Pareto's 80/20 principle which, if applied to building work, implies that 80% of the value of a contract is contained in 20% of

the most expensive activities [46, 47]. If this rule is applied then the site manager could attempt to identify the cost-significant items and through these (approximately 20% of activities) effect control of 80% of total project costs.

(3) Monitor and produce reports based on an exception principle. Only activities exhibiting negative variances are analysed and reported on. This implies that where an activity is partially complete, there is an ability to measure negative variances in the cost data presented. The site manager will require a cost breakdown of each work activity and these cost elements need to be allocated to their relative time positions on the programme. The following example demonstrates the approach:

Example: Activity description – extracted from tender analysis

One brick thick wall in 65 mm common bricks, in cement mortar (1:3) laid in English bond   250 m²   @   25.63
The total activity value = 250 m² × £25.63 = £6407.50

Rate breakdown – taken from the estimator's build-up sheets:

Labour   = 14.85
Materials   =   6.41
Plant   =   0.06
Overheads =   2.15
Profit   =   2.16
                       25.63/m²

Labour content   = £3712.50 (512 production hours)
Material content   = £1602.50 (30 975 bricks including waste)
Plant content   = £15.00
Bricklayer all-in rate = £5.00
Labour all-in rate   = £4.50
Gang   = 2 and 1
Programmed work   = 4 weeks = 148 production hours
                       (37-hour week)
Number of gangs   = 4

Having extracted the above information from the estimate, this can be tabulated for monitoring purposes as illustrated in Figure 11.20. The activity quantities are broken down into programmed units and the estimated cost of the three resources specified by the tender method statement are applied to weekly quantities of work. Actual resource

Project Nr 1   Activity Cost Statement   Month/Week ending:

                                              Date:

Contract Method Statement – 4 Nr 2 and 1 gangs for 4 weeks (37 hr wk)

Wk Nr	Activity	Qty	Unit	Rate	Value	Labour Est. cost	Labour Act. cost	Plant Est. cost	Plant Act. cost	Materials Est. cost	Materials Act. cost	Actual cost total	Margin Tender	Margin Actual
					£	£	£	£	£	£	£	£	£	£
1	1 brick wall in commons	40	m²	25.63	1025.20	594	550	2.40	8.00	256.40	300	858	172.40	167.20
2	"	60	m²	25.63	1537.80	891		3.60		384.60			258.60	
3	"	68	m²	25.63	1742.84	1009.80		4.08		435.88			293.08	
4	"	82	m²	25.63	2101.66	1217.70		4.92		525.62			353.42	
Totals					6407.50	3712.50		15.00		1602.50			1077.50	

Figure 11.20   Site manager's activity cost statement

costs can be compared with estimated costs on a regular basis using allocation and materials received sheets.

The site manager will be interested in three main aspects of each activity cost statement:

(1) Over-/under-spending on individual resource elements and comparing these with programme requirements.
(2) Variance in margin achieved.
(3) Projected cost to complete an activity on time.

Using the information generated within each activity statement, the site manager is able to instigate timely corrective action. Also, if variances in resource costs do arise then the reasons for these can be investigated, e.g. material cost variance could be due to either a price increase or higher wastage levels being experienced.

A report to contracts management

The information from the activity cost statements is now required to be collected and presented in a report for the contract manager's attention, and Figure 11.21 is an illustration of this type of report. The information presented on the operational cost reconciliation statement identifies the current resource cost position and shows where cost variances have occurred.

The site manager should also be in a position to explain any variances and to put forward a course of remedial action when necessary.

The responsibility reporting system

Figure 11.16 illustrates the general principles of the cost reporting system which employs responsibility levels as its theme. It is worth mentioning that in a small building company the general management responsibilities will normally be a board level function. This model is based on the use of standard statements, which can be adapted to the individual needs of companies.

It should also be possible to develop a coded reference system for data at each of the four levels which allows costs at each level to be logically linked and compared.

Summary

The monitoring and control process commences with the analysis of past financial performance. From the analysis and development of the corporate budget a number of key relationships and target criteria can be identified and form important measurement indicators.

Project Nr 1   (amounts in £s)   Operational Cost Reconciliation May 1989   Date: 15 May 1989   Contract time elapsed: 3 months

Operations	Budget cost total	Labour Est. cost	Labour Act. cost	Labour Cost variance	Plant Est. cost	Plant Act. cost	Plant Cost variance	Materials Est. cost	Materials Act. cost	Materials Cost variance	Sub-contractors Est. cost	Sub-contractors Act. cost	Sub-contractors Cost variance	Total Est. cost total	Total Act. cost total	Total variance
[Prelims]	31 500	4 000	5 000	(1 000)	1 250	1 250	—	2 250	3 250	(1 000)	1 000	1 000	—	10 500		
[Site staff]	12 000	3 000	3 000	—					—			—		3 000		
Substructure	25 000	7 500	7 500	—	5 000	5 000	—	12 500	12 500	—	2 000	2 000	—	25 000		
Frame	30 000	500	500	—				1 500	2 500	(1 000)	1 000	1 500	(500)	2 000		
Exterior walls	15 000													1 000		
Interior walls																
Roof																
Services		1 000	1 000	—										1 000		
1st fix (woodwork)																
Finishes																
2nd fix (woodwork)																
Decorations																
External works																
Snagging																
Final clean																
Total	210 000															
Totals to-date		16 000	17 000	(1 000)	6 250	6 250	—	16 250	18 250	(2 000)	4 000	4 500	(500)	42 500	46 000	(3 500)

Figure 11.21 Site manager's operational cost reconciliation

Examples of these are given in the text and are used to develop the structure and integration within initially the corporate budget and then the system as whole.

Allied to the development of the corporate budget is the establishment of a forecast balance sheet, profit statement and a series of management ratios, which represent the company's desired financial objectives.

The corporate budget is the directors' benchmark against which performance data contained in the responsibility reports is compared.

Each contract will be seen to make a contribution, initially to the company's administration costs and then to profit. The measurement of contribution and the time/cost consequences of working capital usage have been taken into account in the development of the corporate budget and are then evaluated within the reporting system.

The responsibility reports are based on a series of control statements which analyse 'cost' and 'value' information to suit responsibility requirements.

At the culmination of a trading period, a series of final trading statements are produced and the company's actual trading performance is compared with the planned performance, which is continually evolving to suit market conditions and is depicted in the control documentation described.

The process then re-commences with the analysis phase in readiness for a future period.

Finally, Figure 11.22 depicts what is an important aspect within the control system and processes, that of linking data used within different accounting systems of companies. If financial information employed for different purposes can be related within an integrated administration system, the results can be used as management decision-making aids with much more confidence.

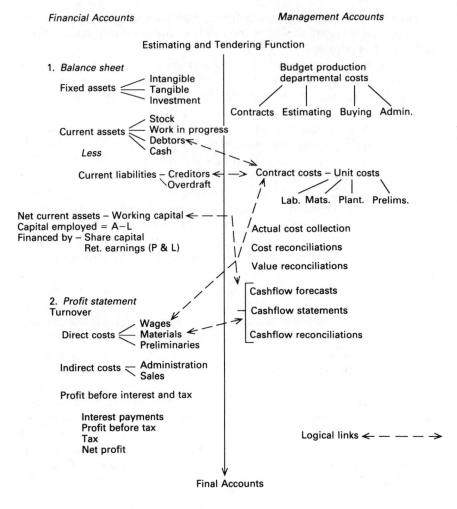

Figure 11.22   Financial control information

References

1. Canter M.R., Cashflow Appraisal and Evaluation for Small Construction Companies, M. Phil. Thesis, CNAA, 1988.
2. Cooke B., *Contract Planning and Contractual Procedures*, Macmillan, 1986.
3. Hillebrandt P.M., Small Firms in the Construction Industry – Committee of Inquiry on Small Firms, Research Report No. 10, HMSO, 1976.
4. Devine P.J., Lee N., Jones R.M. and Tyson W.J., *An Introduction to Industrial Economics*, 4th edn, Allen & Unwin, 1986.
5. *Housing and Construction Statistics – 1976–1985*, Government Statistical Service, 1986.
6. *Construction Forecasts (1984, 1985, 1986)* and *(1987, 1988, 1989)*, N.E.D.O., June 1984 and June 1987.
7. Hillebrandt P.M., *Analysis of the British Construction Industry*, Macmillan, 1984.
8. Hillebrandt P.M., *Economic Theory and the Construction Industry*, Macmillan, 1985.
9. Phelps-Brown E.H., *Report of the Committee of Inquiry Under Prof. E.H. Phelps-Brown into Certain Matters Concerning Labour in Building and Civil Engineering*, Cmnd 3714, HMSO, 1968.
10. Norris K., *Small Building Firms – Their Origins, Characteristics and Development Needs*, Occasional Paper No. 32, CIOB, September 1984.
11. Whitmore D.A., *Work Study and Related Management Services*, Heinemann, 1976.
12. Lucas H., *Companion to Management Studies*, Heinemann, 1982.
13. Humble J., *Improving Management Performance*, B.I.M., 1969.
14. Humble J., *Improving Business Results*, McGraw-Hill, 1967.
15. CIOB, Site Management Checklist No. 1 – Plant Selection and Utilisation, *Building Technology and Management*, January 1986.
16. CIOB, *Code of Estimating Practice*, CIOB, October 1983.

17. Thornton N., *Management Accounting*, Heinemann, 1978.
18. Franks J., *Financial Management for Construction Firms*. A collection of edited articles published in *Building Trades Journal*, January 1979–August 1981.
19. Walmsley K. (Consultant Editor), *Butterworth's Company Law Handbook*, 6th edn, Butterworth, 1987.
20. Archer G., Accounting and Requirements – Standards and Legislation. Presented at a seminar on *Financial Management for Contractors*, CIOB, November 1984.
21. *Statement of Standard Accounting Practice. S.S.A.P.9: Stocks and Work in Progress*, Institute of Chartered Accountants, May 1975.
22. Foster C., *Building with Men*, Tavistock, 1969.
23. CIOB, *The Practice of Estimating*, CIOB, June 1981.
24. Braid, S.R., *Importance of Estimating Feedback*, CIOB, Technical Information Service Paper No. 39, 1984.
25. Barrett F.R. *Cost Value Reconciliation*, CIOB, September 1981.
26. Cooke J.E. and Jepson W.B., *Cost and Financial Control for Construction Firms*, Macmillan, 1979.
27. Cooke J.E., Charting the Course of Progress, *Building*, 3rd October 1980.
28. Harris F. and McCaffer R., *Modern Construction Management*, Granada, 1985.
29. Farzad F., *An Interactive Computer Based Simulation for Budgeting and Forecasting of Construction Project Expenditure Pattern Using a New Model*, South Bank Polytechnic, 1987.
30. Hudson K.W., D.H.S.S. Expenditure Forecasting Method. Presented at Conference on *Financial Policy and Control in Construction Projects*, RICS/ICE/IOB/DOE, May 1980.
31. *Standard Form of Building Contract*, 1980 edn, Joint Contracts Tribunal, 1980.
32. *Intermediate Form of Contract*, 1984 edn, Joint Contracts Tribunal, 1984.
33. Canter M.R., *The Relationship Between Cashflow, Profit and Profitability on Contracts – The Small Builder and his Problems*, Anglia Polytechnic University, 1987.
34. Jones R., All Systems Go, *National Builder*, July/August 1987.
35. Argenti J., Company Failure – Long Range Prediction Not Enough, *Accountancy*, August 1977.
36. Open Access – Integrated Management System, *Software Products International*, 1984.
37. Rockley L.E., *The Meaning of Balance Sheets and Company Reports – A Guide for Non-Accountants*, Business Books, 1983.
38. Rockley L.E., *Finance for the Non-Accountant*, Business Books, 1986.

39. Gibbs J., *A Practical Approach to Financial Management*, Financial Training Publications, 1978.
40. Reynolds P.J. and Hesketh P., An Analysis of the Construction Industry, *Construction Industry Handbook*, M.T.P., Lancaster, 1973.
41. Robertson, G.F., The Problem Examined. Presented at Institute of Building Seminar *Getting Paid*, March 1977.
42. Jones J.R., *Finance and the Control of Cost – Construction Management in Principle and Practice* (edited by E.F.L. Brech), Longman, 1971.
43. Leaflet C.A.I., *Capital Allowance on Machinery or Plant*, H.M. Inspector of Taxes, 1985.
44. Franks J., *Building Procurement Systems*, CIOB, September 1984.
45. Allars P.D., Financial Management for Contractors. Presented at *Chartered Institute of Building Seminar*, November 1984.
46. Jaafari A. and Mateffy B.K., What Every Construction Manager Should Know about Construction Cost Control, *International Journal of Construction Management and Technology*, Vol. 1, No. 1, 1986.
47. Saket M.M., Mackay K.J. and Horner R.M., Some Applications of the Principle of Cost-Significance, *International Journal of Construction Management*, December 1986.

Index